THE RHYTHM BAND BOOK

By RUTH ETKIN

Illustrated by Bunny Cappiello

With photographs by David Cohen

80-59

STERLING
PUBLISHING CO., INC.   NEW YORK

Oak Tree Press Co., Ltd.
London & Sydney

OTHER BOOKS OF INTEREST

Best Singing Games for Children of All Ages
Dancing Games for Children of All Ages
Make Your Own Musical Instruments
Movement Games for Children of All Ages
Musical Games for Children of All Ages
Playing and Composing on the Recorder
Singing & Dancing Games for the Very Young

To my own merry band, Stan, Janet and Elaine, and to my mother and father, in whose home Dorothy, Teddy, Evie and I made beautiful music together.

A special thank you to my editor, Sheila Barry, for sharing her talents and expertise and, especially, for her friendship.

Second Printing, 1979
Copyright © 1978 by Sterling Publishing Co., Inc.
Two Park Avenue, New York, N.Y. 10016
Distributed in Australia by Oak Tree Press Co., Ltd.,
P.O. Box J34, Brickfield Hill, Sydney 2000, N.S.W.
Distributed in the United Kingdom
by Ward Lock Ltd., 116 Baker Street, London W.1
Manufactured in the United States of America
All rights reserved
Library of Congress Catalog Card No.: 78-57886
Sterling ISBN 0-8069-4570-2 Trade   Oak Tree 7061-2605-X
4571-0 Library

CONTENTS

Cheryl, Michael and Huntz are playing in their classroom at school. But they could just as well be playing in the school gym or auditorium. They would sound as good in a park, a back yard, or in the living room at home. One of the great things about playing in a rhythm band is that you can make music almost anywhere with almost anything.

GETTING STARTED

Playing any musical instrument can be fun. It can be even better if you can play the music together with your friends. Playing in a rhythm band is a great way to share music with your friends, because the instruments are easy to play without much practice. Rhythm band instruments are also easy to make with materials found around the house, and you can invent new ones with just a bit of imagination. When you play in a rhythm band, you learn a lot about music—reading and writing it as well as playing it. You can play for yourselves or you can put on concerts. You can even learn to create your own patterns for the band to play.

Many people can play in your band or just a few, but you should have at least 4 players so you can include enough instruments with different sounds; that makes your music more interesting.

There is no special age for rhythm band players. Children as young as 4 or 5 can be part of your band with a little practice. Adults will enjoy being part of your band, too, sometimes. They can play instruments, accompany you on the piano, or conduct the band.

Since these instruments only beat the rhythm of the music, the melody of each song has to be played or sung by someone who can play a melody instrument. The musical scores in this book have been written for piano, but you can play them with a songflute, recorder, or guitar. If you don't have any of these instruments, you can keep the melody going in other ways. You can learn the songs and sing along, or get someone to tape the songs for you on a cassette. Then the music is ready to use when you're ready to play.

The music in this book comes from all over the world. Some of the songs are familiar folktunes; some have been written by famous composers. Other songs are less well-known, but they have unique and interesting rhythms. Some songs are meant to be played very fast, like the marches; some very slow. Every one of them has a good, interesting beat that works especially well for rhythm bands.

INSTRUMENTS OF THE RHYTHM BAND

Rhythm band instruments are all *percussion* instruments. That means that you play them by hitting, striking, scraping or shaking them. They fall into four basic groups:

sticks (for scraping)
triangles (for striking)
tambourines (for shaking)
drums (for hitting)

For a beginning rhythm band, you need at least one of each kind. You can buy them in most music shops and in some toy and department stores. But you can make instruments of your own from supplies you can find around your house or in school.

You can create the sound of rhythm band sticks, for example, with a pair of wooden mixing spoons, pencils or chopsticks. You can make drum sounds by beating on the plastic lids of empty food containers or cannisters. The instruments you make may not reproduce the exact sounds of the store-bought instruments, but you'll come pretty close. And it's fun to make the instruments your band will play.

You'll find directions for making tambourines, triangles, and many other instruments in the song pages throughout the book. The more different kinds of sounds you can get, the more interesting your band will sound. In fact, even if you can get a set of ready-made rhythm band instruments, it's still a good idea to make your own. It doubles your enjoyment.

Sticks
smooth

grooved

Thin cylinders of wood about 12 inches (30 cm) long, used in pairs. You play by striking the smooth sticks together. If you have sticks that come with grooves, you can strike them together, crossed, or rub them together.

Tambourine

A circular, wooden instrument, about 6–10 inches (15–25 cm) in diameter and 2 inches (5 cm) deep. The top of the tambourine is covered with parchment, and metal discs are spaced along the wooden sides. These discs jingle when you hit the parchment with the flat of your hand (or on your knee, for special effects). You get another kind of sound if you shake the tambourine. To make your own, see page 30.

Triangle

A three-sided metal instrument from 4–10 inches (10–25 cm) high, attached to a cord. You hold the cord in one hand (to allow the triangle to vibrate) and hit the triangle gently with a metal "striker" held in your other hand. To make your own, see page 50.

Drum

You can use many kinds of drums. Most common is the circular wooden drum, about 8–10 inches (20–25 cm) in diameter and 6–7 inches (15–18 cm) deep, covered top and bottom by parchment. You hit it with 1 or 2 wooden drumsticks or with the flat of your hand. You can make other kinds of drums (see pages 50 and 85).

EXTRAS FOR THE BAND

Sand Blocks

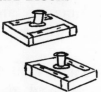

A pair of wooden squares or rectangles about 4 × 4 inches (10 × 10 cm) or 3 × 5 inches (7 × 13 cm), with wooden knobs or handles. The playing surface is covered with rough-grained sandpaper. You play them by rubbing the sandpaper sides against each other. To make your own, see page 90. When you play, follow the tambourine part.

Claves

Pairs of wooden sticks, cylindrical and about 6–7 inches (15–18 cm) long and 1–2 inches (2–5 cm) in diameter. You play them by cupping one of them in your hand lengthwise and hitting it with the other, which you hold lengthwise right above it. You can get another effect by hitting them together crossed, the way you do with the sticks.

Guiro

Most often used in Africa and Latin America, the guiro is wooden and oval shaped, with grooves running around it. You play by scraping a small wooden stick along the grooves.

Wood Blocks

A hollow, wooden cylinder about 4–5 inches (10–13 cm) long on a handle. Hit it with a wooden mallet and it makes a hollow sound quite different from the sticks or claves.

Cymbals

Brass instruments, circular and 4–8 inches (10–20 cm) in diameter, with wooden handles. Play them in pairs by hitting glancing blows, one against the other, allowing the cymbals to vibrate. For another kind of sound—more like a Chinese Gong (see page 75)—hit one of them with a wooden mallet or a drumstick. Follow the drum part when you play, but use them sparingly.

Finger Cymbals

Similar to regular cymbals, but only about 2–3 inches (5–7 cm) wide, these are delicate and quiet relatives of the larger cymbals. They tinkle when you hit them together.

Bells

"Sleigh bells" attached to strips of canvas about 1 inch (2 cm) wide. You can sew the ends of the canvas tape together to make a "bracelet" for easy handling. If you want a hollow, ringing sound, try cowbells, with their large 4–5 inch (10–13 cm), heavy metal bodies and metal clappers.

Jingle Sticks

Round sticks about 6 inches (15 cm) long, with metal discs attached to a round wooden circle at the top of the stick. When you shake them, the discs jingle against the circle. Follow the bells part when you play.

EXTRAS FOR THE BAND (Continued)

Jingle Rattles

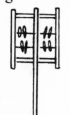

Sticks, about 13 inches (33 cm) long with cross bars to which 4 pairs of metal discs are attached. Add them when you want lots of jangling sounds.

Bell Shakers

Similar to a tambourine, but easier to handle. These are made from wooden sticks or dowels. Attach bells or metal discs by threading a cord through the opening of each disc, forming a loop. Then nail the loops to the stick, spacing them evenly from top to bottom, but leaving room to hold the shaker. The more bells, the more sound.

Maracas

gourds

You can make these Latin American maracas from papier-mâché shaped into round balls. Leave a small hole at the bottom of each ball. When it is dry, fill the ball with dried seeds or rice or beans. Insert a handle (pencil or dowel stick) into the hole. Tape the handle to keep it attached securely and to seal in the "shaking material." You can make maracas with dried gourds, too. These are vegetables whose seeds produce a shaking sound after drying out for 3–4 weeks. Insert handles, following the directions above. Shake the maracas crisply—singly or in pairs—

to get a 1-beat sound. Shake them continuously and you get a different sound.

Shakers

Plastic cylinders, 12–13 inches (30–33 cm) long and filled with sand, they make a sand-block type of sound when you shake them. Often the shaker is used as a partner to sand blocks, especially when you want a more distinct, wave-like quality. You can shake 2 at a time and add even more of the sand-in-motion sound.

Seed Pods

Large, dried seed pods, 12 inches (30 cm) long or more, usually of the tropical poinciana tree. They are a popular accompaniment to African and Latin American music. The dried seeds inside make an interesting sound when you shake them. You can also use smaller pods, less than half that size. Dried pods of the locust tree (which grows in more temperate climates) sound similar.

As you add instruments, follow the rhythm pattern for a similar instrument. With claves and wood blocks, for example, you'd play the score for the sticks. Bells of all kinds fit in with triangles. Some of the instruments you collect or create may not fit into any group. In that case, follow any pattern you want or create a new one of your own. Do what comes naturally to you as the band plays.

Store-Bought Instruments: (Foreground) *jingle rattle.* (Front row) *tambourine; jingle stick; sticks; claves; sand blocks; cymbals; finger cymbals; bells.* (Back row) *drum; triangle with striker; shaker; wood block with mallet; guiro with scraper inserted; seed pod; maracas.*

Home-Made Instruments: (Front row) *pie-plate tambourine with spool handle; ring-box castanets; sand blocks made from sandpaper-covered wood pieces with spool handles; tambourine made from plastic coffee can lid with bells; finger cymbals from keys; flower pot tambour; frying pan gong.* (Back row) *"blowing" jugs; box guitar; shaker made from a rice-filled paper "envelope" on an ice-cream stick; finger cymbals made from candle holders; oatmeal box drum covered with foil; milk container shaker filled with dry macaroni; kazoo made from a toilet tissue paper core covered with waxed paper; wooden box string instrument (like the koto or dulcimer); guiro made from a tray covered with rows of heavy string. Behind the guiro is a shaker made from a plastic jug filled with dry rice, and an oatmeal box drum decorated with paper cut-outs.*

HOW TO READ THE SCORES

The *score* for each song has been set up so that it's easy for you to follow it. You'll see the melody on the left-hand page. The "rhythm band" score is on the right-hand page. Each *measure* of the melody is matched by a measure of rhythm band suggestions. Moving measure by measure, you can follow the pattern of the instrument you are playing and match it to the melody.

In order to read the rhythm band score, you need to know what each symbol stands for. Look over this sample and the explanation that follows, and you'll be able to see what each mark tells you to do.

4 The number at the beginning of each score tells you how many beats there are in each measure of the music. It matches the *time signature* in the music on the left-hand page.

X — Picture symbol for the *sticks*.

△ — Picture symbol for the *triangle*.

— Picture symbol for the *tambourine*.

— Picture symbol for the *drum*.

— Picture symbol for the *maracas*.

— Picture symbol for the *finger cymbals*.

— Picture symbol for the *coconut halves*.

— Picture symbol for the *cymbals*.

— Picture symbol for the *bells*.

— Picture symbol for *African drums*.

— Picture symbol for the *guiro*.

— Picture symbol for the *castanets*.

♩– *Play once* on this beat of the measure.

♫ *Play twice* on this beat of the measure.

♩ *Play* this beat *louder* or with more force.

𝄽 A *rest* symbol. Do not play on this beat.

ⱳ *Shake* the instrument on the beat, rather than strike it. This is often used for instruments like the tambourine or maracas.

| The *bar line* separates each measure of the score. Each set of beats counts as a new measure.

* The *pick-up measure* is not a full measure. It leads into the first full-count measure. The number of beats in the pick-up measure added to the number of beats in the last measure of a song always total a full measure's beats.

This *double bar line* indicates that the song is completed.

This *repeat sign* tells you to play the previous section or the whole song over again. Whatever comes before the repeat sign is repeated.

D.C. al Fine: This tells you to repeat from the beginning of the song until the place marked *Fine*. It is an abbreviation of the Latin phrase *Da cap al Fine* (from the head to the end).

Once you master the rhythm patterns, the next step is to vary them in your own way. As you play, you can use your own ideas to invent rhythms that add a different and original flavor to the music.

CREATING YOUR OWN RHYTHM BAND SCORES

Once you have the feel of adding new instruments and creating new rhythms, you can begin to mark down your own inventions. When you put your ideas on paper, you have a permanent record of the new rhythm patterns. That way you'll be able to recreate a pattern you've developed and enjoyed. Also, your friends will be able to read your new rhythm ideas when they play and can join you easily.

To keep a record of your new patterns, follow the same system that you see in the side-by-side scores in this book.

Take blank paper the same size as the page with the melody you will accompany. Draw your rhythm score to match the melody score, setting down the same number of bar lines in the rhythm score that you have in the melody. If you're going to be able to follow the music easily, your rhythm band lines need to be the same size as the melody lines.

When your paper is set up, write in the rhythm pattern for one instrument at a time. Use the symbols to show when to play and when to be still. By singing the melody to yourself (or playing it) as you develop your own patterns, you'll be able to keep the rhythm score matching the melody. Or you can get someone to tape the melody for you in advance and use the tape to keep your rhythm matching correctly. You can also get a friend to play parts of the melody again and again until you have the rhythm just right. This is important because you want both parts—the melody and the rhythm score—to move together.

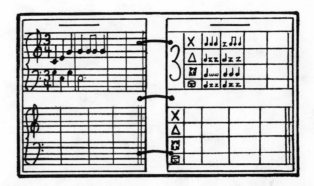

Before you make your score marks permanent, be sure to play through each line so that it's exactly the way you want it. As composer and arranger, you need to check the music many times so that other people will be able to play it accurately and as beautifully as you planned it.

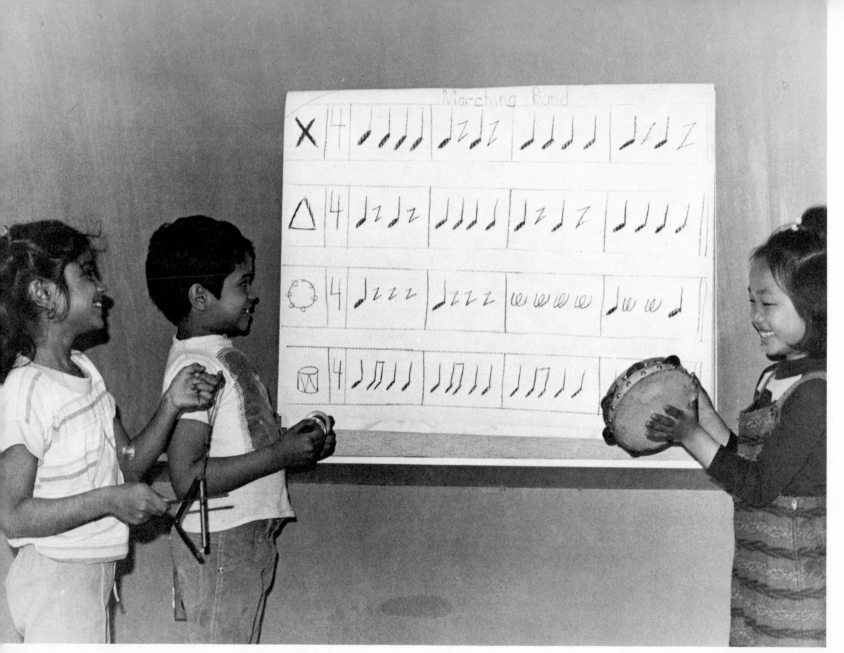

You can make a giant-size score with large oaktag sheets about 22 × 26 inches (56 × 66 cm). You can also use "butcher paper," cut to that size from a roll you get from a stationery store. If you hang up those sheets, they will be seen clearly by everyone.

HOW TO CONDUCT YOUR RHYTHM BAND

After you practice some of the music with your friends, you might want to play together like a professional band. You might want to give a performance for your family, friends or school. A professional band usually works under the leadership of a *conductor*.

The conductor sets the pace of the music—faster or slower—and keeps the rhythm steady so that all the band members stay together.

You and your friends can take turns conducting the band. Either use your hand to conduct or a *baton*. A pencil or dowel makes a good substitute, if you don't have a real baton. Whatever you use, stand where all the players can see you. It is easier for everyone—players and conductor—if all those playing the same kind of instrument sit together. It's a good idea to have a copy of the score for each player. It takes just a little practice to keep an eye on both the score and conductor.

There are several conducting patterns that you'll want to learn. They follow the rhythm of the music so perfectly that it is easy to conduct—and easy to follow a conductor—once you learn them.

The patterns shown here are the ones you'll need most often for the music in this book and for most of the music you'll choose to play on your own.

To conduct a song that *counts in 4* (4/4 *time signature*) follow the arrow marks and lead a set of 4 counts:

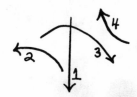

To conduct a song that *counts in 3* (3/4 time signature) follow this set of arrows:

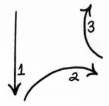

To conduct a song that *counts in 2* (2/4 or 2/2 time signature), follow these arrows with your hand:

To make it easy for the players to start exactly on time, most conductors give the band an *upbeat*. That means that before you bring your hand down on the first strong beat (beat #1 in each measure), swing your arm up, as these arrows show, so the players have time to get ready.

Some players find it easier to start if the conductor conducts a full measure before they begin to play. It helps them feel how fast or slow the conductor will be counting. You might want to try that, too, especially at the beginning.

IF YOU'RE HAPPY AND YOU KNOW IT

American folksong

This is a good song to start with, because it's so familiar. Sing it as your band plays, and add a new idea each time. Start with "stamp your feet," but the next time through you can "nod your head," "twirl around," "jump up high," "wrinkle your nose"—whatever you can do while you play your instrument.

After that you can turn this into a singing game for

instruments. Call for individual instruments to play, like this:

"If you're happy and you know it, play the sticks." Then the sticks play solo, in rhythm, where song says "Stamp, stamp." You can see in the rhythm score that the tambourine and the drum have parts to play

IF YOU'RE HAPPY AND YOU KNOW IT

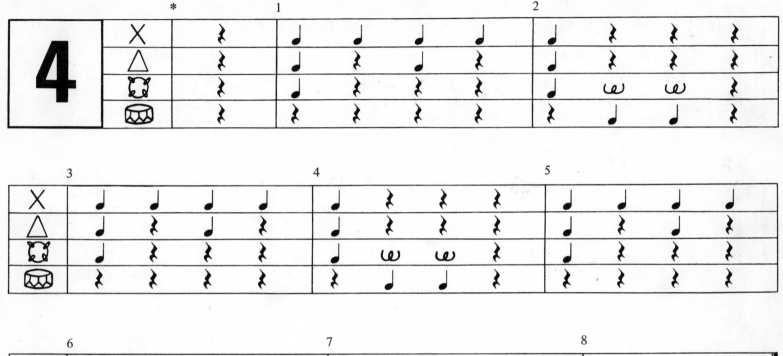

there, but in this game you play only the called-for instrument in those places.

Next you can try, "If you're happy and you know it, beat the drum," or "ring the bells," or even lines that don't fit so well:

tap the tambourine   crash the cymbals
try the triangles   shake the shakers

After each instrument has had a turn to play alone, you can have a *grand finale* (an important-sounding end to the song):

"If you're happy and you know it, play them all!" and finish with a loud, happy sound.

I AM A FINE MUSICIAN

English folksong

This old English children's song gives you the chance to use many kinds of instruments. As the words say, each instrument must be introduced with a rhyme. Then the instrument plays a *solo* part, in rhythm, from "Boom, boom" to the end of the song.

To make this song move along, you need to make up some good instrument rhymes in advance. You might want to sing:

I am a fine musician,
I'm known both near and far.
And I can play sweet music
Upon my brown guitar.

Remember, you'll have to follow the rhythm:
I am a fine musician,
— — — — — — —.
And I can play sweet music
Upon my — — — —.

I AM A FINE MUSICIAN

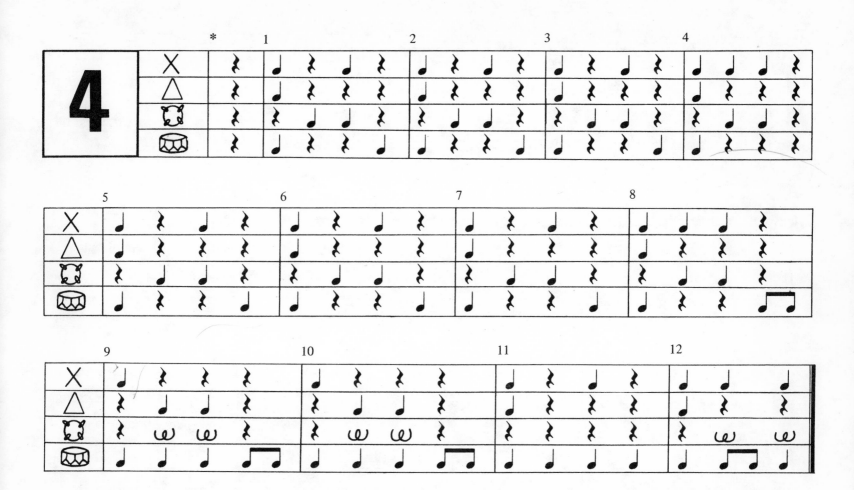

You can create rhymes like *jingle-jangle/triangle* or *tricks/sticks* or *swell/bell*. Anything you can think of that fits the pattern is fine. Silly is just as good as serious.

You can play "pretend" instruments, too, even if you don't have them in your band. You can imitate their sounds instead. You can rhyme things like *marshmallow/cello* or *clone/trombone*.

You can go further and use your imagination to invent your own instrument sounds by rhyming things like *Mabel/table*, playing your solo part on the nearest desk. Or you could rhyme *balloon/spoon*, tapping a spoon in your palm. Create a rhyme for anything that produces a sound, and you can make this song go on for a long, enjoyable time.

OLD McDONALD HAD A BAND

Classic children's song

Old Mc - Don - ald had a band E - I - E - I - O. And

in that band he had a drum E - I - E - I - O. With a

boom, boom here and a boom, boom there, Here a boom, there a boom, Ev-'ry-where a boom, boom,

Old Mc - Don - ald had a band E - I - E - I - O.

OLD McDONALD HAD A BAND

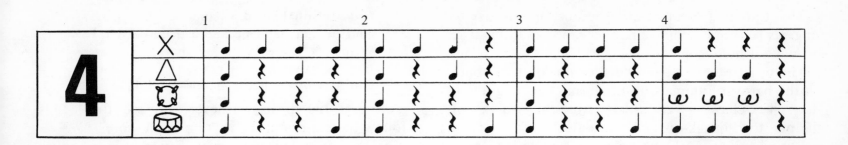

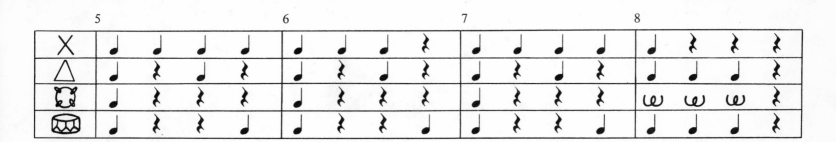

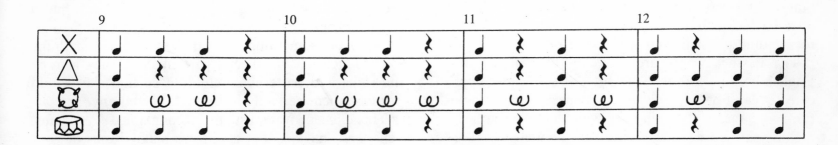

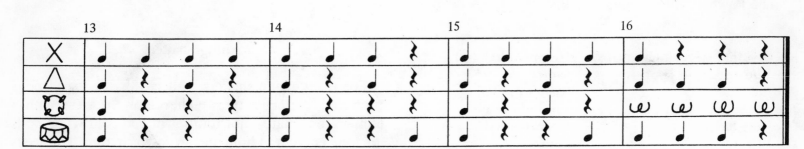

OLD McDONALD HAD A BAND

This tune is a great favorite because it's so easy to sing. Its pattern is simple, and you can keep it that way or make it more complicated.

The usual way to sing "Old McDonald" tells about all the barnyard animals on the farm. You sing about the "chick-chick" of the chicken, the "oink-oink" of the pig, the "quack-quack" of the duck.

But when Mr. McDonald is a music-loving farmer, you have a brand new song for your rhythm band.

Your words can go something like this:

Old McDonald had a band—E I E I O.
And in that band he had a drum—E I E I O.
With a * * here and a * * there,
Here a * there a * ev'rywhere a * *
Old McDonald had a band—E I E I O.

You beat the drum whenever you see the *. Just follow the pattern in the rhythm band score.

Sing enough stanzas to give every instrument a turn. Follow the singing pattern of the song and repeat all the old instruments each time you add a new one.

TO THE SUN

The Pawnee Indians were one of the Great Buffalo Hunting Tribes of the plains of the midwestern United States. This morning prayer is a chant that was part of a Pawnee ritual "thanksgiving" to the Sky Father for sending the light and warmth of the sun.

The Pawnee words are not easy to translate into English because a short word often describes a complicated idea. For example, the Pawnee word "rah-wi-rah-ri-se" means "walking the wide earth beneath the arching sky," a way they described themselves.

The Pawnee words sound like this:

If you look at the musical score, you'll find the same rhythmic beat repeated all through the chant. This is typical of American Indian dances. Each dance had a special purpose: asking for something, praying to be spared from something, or thanksgiving for something. Each dance had its special participants. They learned the steps and patterns as children so that they could perform them perfectly in the ritual ceremony.

The dancers were usually accompanied by drums, bells, and shakers. If you want to make drums of your own, take a look at the directions on pages 50 and 85.

Making Shakers

For ready-made shakers, collect the dried seed pods produced by locust trees. (They grow in areas with a temperate climate—not too hot or too cold.) The pods are long enough to hold and shake in rhythm. The seeds inside them, once they dry out (a week or so after they

Hee-ree, ha!	which means	Hearken, ha!
Sha-koo-roo, wah rook-stay		Sacred sun
Kah-tah, ha!		Rising up, ha!
Tee-rah-rah-wah-hut, ha!		Circle in heaven, ha!
Hee-ree, ha!		Hearken, ha!
Tee-rah-wah,		Supreme God,
Hee-ree, ha!		Hearken, ha!

Brett is holding the bells in his hands and shaking them as he moves. Dana (center) is wearing her bells as bracelets and allowing them to shake freely as she dances around the circle. You can't see her feet, but Stephanie (left) is wearing the bells as cuffs. As she shuffles her feet, step by step, the bells keep a steady jingling beat. This leaves her hands free to clap or snap or to carry shakers or other instruments.

TO THE SUN

From a Pawnee chant

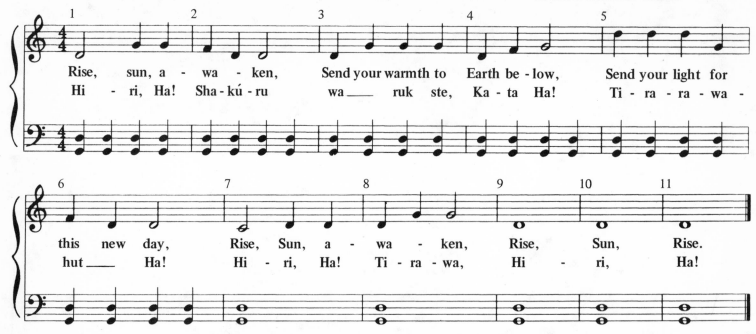

Rise, sun, a - wa - ken, Send your warmth to Earth be - low, Send your light for
Hi - ri, Ha! Sha - kú - ru wa __ ruk ste, Ka - ta Ha! Ti - ra - ra - wa -

this new day, Rise, Sun, a - wa - ken, Rise, Sun, Rise.
hut __ Ha! Hi - ri, Ha! Ti - ra - wa, Hi - ri, Ha!

fall from the tree), bounce back and forth inside the pods, making a scratchy soft sound.

Or if you grow gourds or can get them from the vegetable section of your supermarket, let them dry out for a few weeks. No matter what their size or shape, gourds make a very good shaking sound.

seed pod   *gourds*

Another way to make shakers: fill any kind of container with dried beans, seeds, macaroni or rice. You can use small baby food jars, empty half-pint milk or juice containers, empty plastic bottles from beads or glitter, vitamins or medicine. Decorate them, fill them about half full, and shake.

Making Dancing Cuffs

Get some bells from a pet or toy store. Attach them to a ribbon or elastic tape large enough to tie around your ankles and/or wrists.

TO THE SUN

Then, as you dance and move your arms, the bells will move in rhythm.

You can also make the cuffs by using old, worn-out socks. Cut the cuffs from four of these socks and attach the bells around each of them. Then slip the cuffs over your wrists and ankles. They will stay comfortably in place throughout the dance.

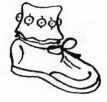

Doing the Sun Dance

Form a circle, facing counter-clockwise. Each dancer should have a pair of shakers (or maracas), if possible.

MEASURES
1 Without lifting your feet from the floor, shuffle forward—right, left, right, left.
2 With your right foot: step on your toe, bring down your heel. Then do it with your left foot.
3 & 4 Repeat 1 & 2.
5 & 6 With your arms in the air, shaking them on each beat, step and hop on your right foot, then left.
7 & 8 Repeat 1 & 2.
9 Raise your arms and shake them 4 times.
10 Standing in place with your knees straight, bend at the waist, arms down, and shake 4 times.
11 Repeat 9.

ALL AROUND THE KITCHEN

American folksong

ALL AROUND THE KITCHEN

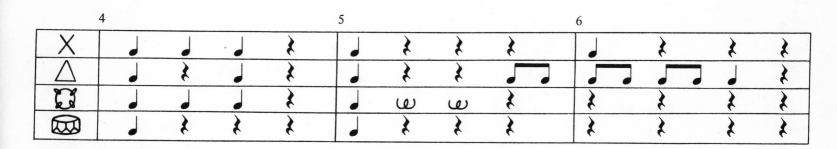

ALL AROUND THE KITCHEN

This play-party game from the southern United States is a musical Follow-the-Leader game. While the band plays the rhythm score, form a line with some of your friends—one behind the other—behind you. Ask the players to place their hands on the shoulders or waist of the person in front. Then, as the band plays, march around the room (the "kitchen") in rhythm, to the words, "All around the kitchen, cock-a-doodle-doodle-doo."

When you get to the words, "And you stop right here, cock-a-doodle-doodle-doo," stop marching and drop hands. When the words tell you, "Do this trick, cock-a-doodle-doodle-doo," you, the line leader, must do something for the others to follow.

You can clap your hands, stamp your feet, swing around, or anything at all that the others can do with you. At the end of the song, go to the end of the line.

The next person now becomes the line leader and a new game begins.

If you want to play this as an instrument game, your rhythm band can march "all around the kitchen" as it plays. When you come to Measure 7, instead of "Do this trick," you, the line leader, sing, "Play the sticks," and you play them solo on the "Cock-a-doodle-doodle-doo" that follows. You'll see that the rhythm band score gives these beats to the triangle, but when you play the instrument game, that part belongs to the line leader's instrument only. Then the next player becomes line leader and gets to call for his or her own instrument and play it.

March around as many times as it takes for each instrument to have a turn as line leader.

COME TO MY FARM

This folksong from Argentina tells about a visit to a farm—much like Old McDonald's farm. You can sing it in English or Spanish and have fun with the animal sounds, make it into a band game or do a circle dance to it.

Just sing it at first. Be sure to notice where the animal sounds (or band sounds) come in: on the last 2 beats of Measure 11 and the first beat of Measure 12; then again on the last 2 beats of Measure 15 and the first beat of Measure 16. You may want to make the animal

sounds solo, even though the rhythm band score shows instruments playing on those beats. Just agree ahead of time and fix your rhythm score to match.

Here are more animal names to sing in Spanish:

   el burrito (boo-REE-toe)—the donkey (burro)
   el patito (pah-TEE-toe)—the duck
   el chanchito (chan-CHEE-toe)—the pig
   el gatito (gah-TEE-toe)—the cat
   el perrito (peh-REE-toe)—the dog

The maracas players are taking their turn in the band game version of Come to My Farm; *Robert and Stephanie are keeping an eye on them. The others are watching the conductor so they will know just when to play. After each section has had a solo turn, they'll all play together from the score on page 29. The other members of the group will dance along and get their chance to do some solo steps.*

COME TO MY FARM

Argentine folksong

COME TO MY FARM

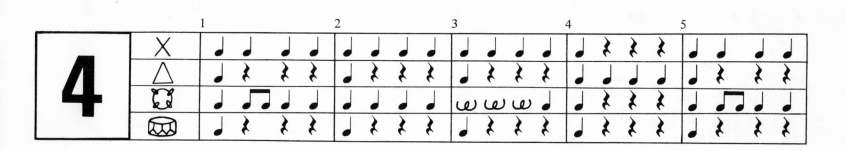

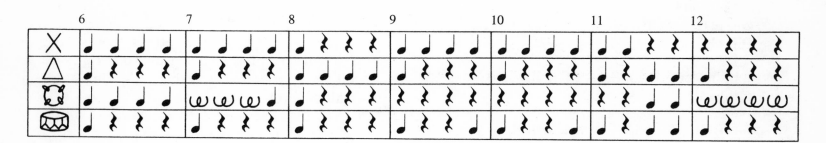

COME TO MY FARM (Continued)

If you want to play this as a band game, just change the words a little. Instead of inviting friends to visit your farm, invite them to play in your band:

MEASURES

1–8   Play in my band with me today.
       Oh, play with me. (Repeat these lines)
9–16   We will shake the tambourine. (drum, etc.)
       (Repeat this line)
17–24 Play, little friend,
       Oh, play, little friend,
       Oh, play with me today. (Repeat)

This same melody becomes a circle dance. Change the words, like this:

Come dance with me, my little friend,
Oh, dance with me. (Repeat these lines)

Let's all dance and stamp our feet, (Repeat)

Come, little friend, oh, come little friend,
Oh, come, oh, come, oh, come. (Repeat these two lines)

Circle Dance

Form a circle, holding hands.

MEASURES

1 & 2 Walk into the circle in rhythm.
3 & 4 Walk backwards to your place.
5 & 6 Repeat 1 & 2.
7 & 8 Repeat 3 & 4.
9 & 10 Stand in place.
11 & 12 Stamp (or dance, or snap or nod) 3 times.
13–16 To the left (clockwise): slide, together, slide, in rhythm. (Give the move a little zip by sliding on your left foot, but stepping on your right *toe* as you bring your feet together. It's almost like a small gallop.)
17–20 Do the same thing to the right (slide with your right foot, step on the toe of your left foot).

Everyone can take turns inventing new things to do when you get to measures 11 and 12. You can blink your eyes, touch your toes, lead the band—even ride the carousel or swim around the pool—whatever you want—as long as you keep to the 1–2–3 rhythm.

TAM TAMBOURINE

The jingling of the tambourine is an important part of the score. As you can see, you'll be playing the tambourine on every beat *except* the first beat in each measure. This is an unusual rhythm pattern, and it calls special attention to the tambourine.

Making a Tambourine

You can make a tambourine from aluminum or metal pie tins. You could even use an embroidery hoop or the plastic covers from coffee cans. Collect things that jingle when you shake them against each

TAM TAMBOURINE (Continued)

other. You can use metal buttons, tiny bells, or the little pull-tabs that open metal soda cans.

*A hoop tambourine—
you shake it.*

*A pie-tin tambourine—
you hit it or shake it.*

Attach as many of these things as you can to the outer rims of the pie tins. Just sew 4 or 5 stitches through, if you're using aluminum plates or plastic lids. Thread the jangles and tie them around if you're using the embroidery hoop. With hard metal plates, use tape to attach the jangles. The more noisemakers you attach, the better the sound will be.

Adding strips of ribbon or colored yarn to the rim of your tambourine will give it a bright, festive look.

Do you recognize the melody? You may already know it in a different version as the story of "My Hat."

Rhythm Band My Hat

**My hat, it has 3 corners,
Three corners has my hat,
And had it not 3 corners,
It would not be my hat.**

You've probably already worked a fingerplay to this song. You start by singing the song through once. The second time you sing it, you *point to yourself* instead of saying the word "my" every time you come to it.

Then you sing the song again, but you not only *point to yourself* instead of singing "my," but you also *touch the top of your head* every time you come to the word "hat," instead of singing it.

Next time you replace the word "three," by holding up 3 fingers each time, also leaving out "my" and "hat." Next you replace the word "corners," as well.

These are the words you replace with gestures:

my: point to yourself.
hat: touch the top of your head.
three: hold up 3 fingers.
corners: form a triangle of the fingers of both hands.

But when you do "My Hat" with your rhythm band, you let the instruments take the part of your fingers. Choose an instrument to replace each of the words. The drum could be "my," the triangle "hat"—whatever

TAM TAMBOURINE

Italian folksong

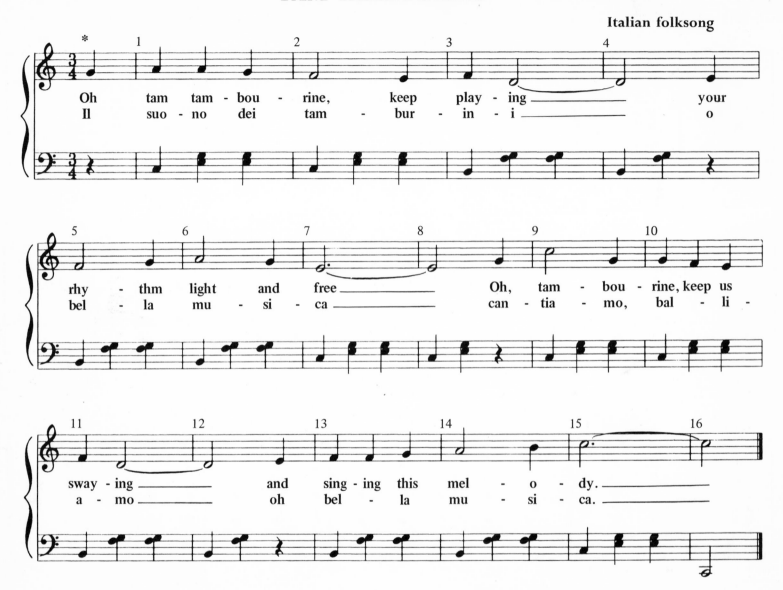

Oh tam tam-bou - rine, keep play - ing _____ your
Il suo - no dei tam - bur - in - i _____ o

rhy - thm light and free _____ Oh, tam - bou - rine, keep us
bel - la mu - si - ca _____ can - tia - mo, bal - li -

sway - ing _____ and sing - ing this mel - o - dy. _____
a - mo oh bel - la mu - si - ca. _____

you choose. Then, as you sing the song, play the instrument instead of gesturing on the left-out word.

The last part of the game might go like this:

Drum	Triangle	**it has**	Sticks	Tambourine,
Sticks	Tambourine	**has**	Drum	Triangle,
And had it not		Sticks	Tambourine,	
It would not be		Drum	Triangle.	

TAM TAMBOURINE

If you want to use the rhythm band score, and other instruments are playing along, let the four gesture-instruments step away from the band so they can be heard clearly.

Start slowly until you get used to the actions and fitting in the instruments on time. As you get better, try it faster and faster. Sometimes it's as much fun getting mixed up as getting it right!

Dance Arabi *sets a mood that Patrick (center) has caught perfectly. The girls are smiling at a dancer across the circle who has hung a set of classroom keys on his middle finger. Its tinkling "finger cymbal" sound follows the rhythm beautifully as the dancers step, hop and jump.*

DANCE ARABI

You can add a Middle Eastern touch to this song by using finger cymbals. If you don't have a store-bought pair, you can get a similar sound by using an ordinary pair of keys.

Making Finger Cymbals

Tie a piece of yarn or elastic band through each key so it will move and vibrate as you play it. Hold the keys by the strings and strike them together in rhythm. With a little practice, you can get more sound by using 2 pairs of keys. Hold a pair in each hand, by the strings, and shake them so that they make a tinkling sound.

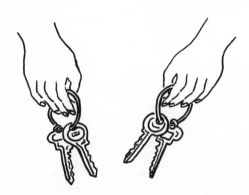

Since different keys are made of different metals, it's a good idea to experiment with the keys you've collected until you find the sounds that please you most. If you can't find two keys that you like together, you can use a single key. Get a nail and hit it against the key with the best tone.

You can do an old folk dance to this melody. It's a simple dance done in a circle by young and old.

Doing the Circle Dance

Form a circle, holding hands with those on either side of you, arms up in the air (see photo on page 34).

MEASURES

1   Hop on your left foot as you tap your right heel, toe pointed up, on the floor. Then do the same thing with your other foot. Hop on your right foot as you tap your left heel.

2   Step backwards: left foot, right foot.

3   Jump with both feet, in place.
     (Repeat 1–3)

4   Step to the left with your left foot. Put your right foot behind your left and step on it. Step to the left again with your left foot, put your right foot behind your left foot and step on it, as before.

5   Jump forward on both feet. Jump back to place on both feet.

6   Step to the right with your right foot. Put your left foot behind your right and step on it. Step to the right again with your right foot, put your left foot behind your right and step on it (Measure 4 in reverse).

DANCE ARABI

Folksong from Egypt

Hey, yah, let us dance a - round, Hey, yah,
Hey, yah, oo - or oh ___ soo, Hey, yah,

let the bells re - sound. Hap - py all to - geth - er, Sing with joy - ful
ed - ra - boo - el garas. Yah - leh neh - frah Ka - wl, Yah - leh neh - frah

voice. Broth - ers here to - geth - er, Let us all re - joice.
Kawl. Ka - wl - ay - nah mah - bahd, Kawl ay - nah mahr bahd.

7   Jump forward on both feet. Jump back to place.

8–11 Repeat 4–7.

Repeat from the beginning at least once more through. As you repeat this dance, it develops a kind of hypnotic feeling that is typical of Middle Eastern

DANCE ARABI

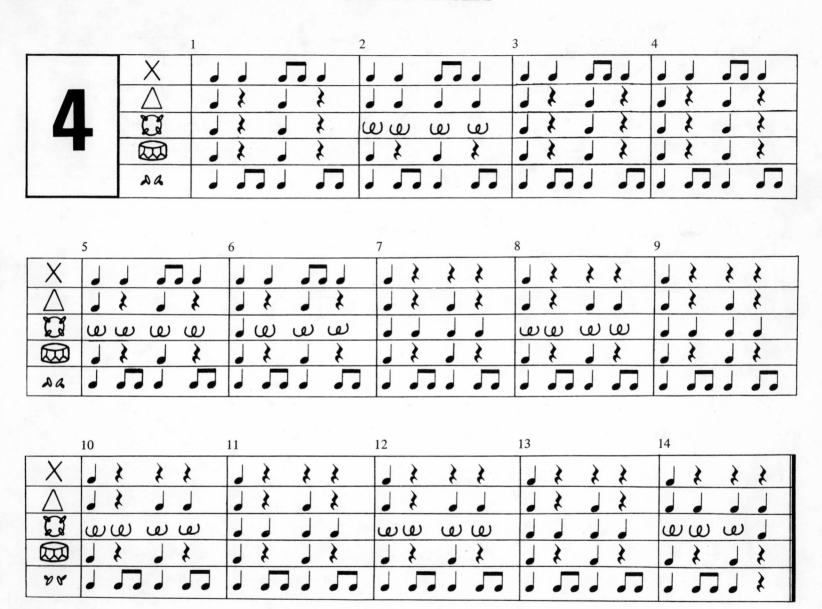

dances. Start out slowly and gradually get faster and
faster until the group is tired enough to agree to stop.

HERE COMES THE JAZZ BAND

Here is a special kind of rhythm called *syncopation*. This is an important rhythm in music today, and it's lots of fun to play. With other rhythm patterns, you get used to the first beat of each measure being the *strong* beat. But notice that in this song, there is a 𝄽 (a rest symbol) at the beginning of many measures.

This "off-the-first-beat" rhythm is what is called syncopation. It helps give jazz its distinctive sound.

The rhythm band scores show 𝄽 (rest marks) for most of the instruments in the first-beat places. This allows a pair of cymbals or a drum to be heard loud and clear. They play while the others are silent.

HERE COMES THE JAZZ BAND

It's important for these instruments to come right in on time. When everyone else is quiet, and the cymbals or drums come in sharply on that "syncopated beat," their solo sound accentuates the "off-the-first-beat" rhythm and makes the number a lively one.

You may want to add some loud metal-clanging chimes to join in with the cymbals in the rhythm band score. Gather together frying pans or skillets of various sizes. The size and composition of the pans will determine the particular tone, but whatever pans you use, you'll get a loud, ringing, jazz-band sound.

TUM BALALAIKA

This version by the Sjeka family

Jewish folksong

1 2 3 4 5 6 7 8
Maid - en, maid - en, will you ex - plain What can grow, ___ grow with-out rain?

9 10 11 12 13 14 15 16
What _ can burn for years _ and years, What _ can cry, cry with - out tears?

Chorus

17 18 19 20 21
Tum - ba - la, tum - ba - la, tum - ba - la - lai - ka, Tum - ba - la,

22 23 24 25 26 27
tum - ba - la, tum - ba - la - lai - ka. Tum - ba - la - lai - ka, Play, ba - la -

turn the page →

TUM BALALAIKA

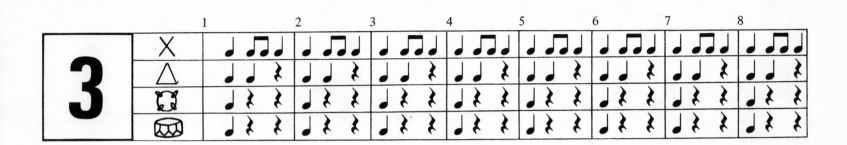

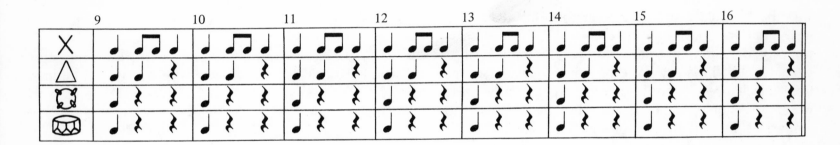

TUM BALALAIKA (Continued)

lai - ka, tum - ba - la - lai - ka, Play me a song.

The part of Europe shared by Poland and Russia was the birthplace of this Jewish folksong. Boys and girls had few opportunities to choose their own partners for any occasion in traditional Jewish families long ago. This is the story of a young man who has the unusual chance to choose one girl from a crowd. He wants to choose someone, but he doesn't want to embarrass himself or any of the girls. He solves his problem by posing some riddles. The girl who answers his questions most cleverly becomes his choice.

The boy strums a balalaika as he sings his riddle song. The balalaika is a 3-stringed instrument with a triangular body. It is still played today in Russia and Poland.

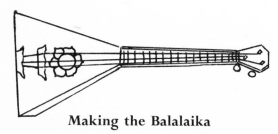

Making the Balalaika

You can make your own balalaika from an empty wooden box about 8–10 inches (20–25 cm) × 6–8 inches (15–20 cm). A cigar box is about the right size. Cut a hole about 3–4 inches (7–10 cm) in diameter out of the top or the bottom. Seal the cover with strong tape (vinyl tape, electrician's tape, or the kind used to seal cartons).

For the neckpiece of the instrument, use a piece of wood about 3–4 inches (7–10 cm) wide by $\frac{1}{4} - \frac{1}{2}$ an inch ($\frac{1}{2} - 1$ cm) deep and 12–14 inches (30–35 cm) long. Nail it to the underside of the balalaika body.

An authentic balalaika is not box-shaped. To get away from that box-like look and make your instrument seem more authentic, decorate it before you string it. If your box has writing on it, paint it or cover it with construction paper. Start your design by taping or pasting a large triangle of a darker or contrasting color on the body. Then color or paint softer-looking designs on the parts outside the triangle. The decoration won't affect the sound of the instrument at all, but it certainly will make it better to look at.

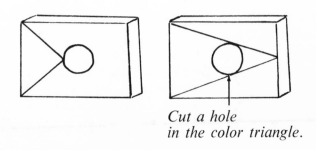

Cut a hole
in the color triangle.

	28	29	30	31	32	33

(Percussion notation for X, triangle, tambourine, and drum across measures 28–33)

String the balalaika with 3 lengths of twine, wire, or elastic bands. Wrap them completely around the instrument—from the top of the neckpiece across the body (right over the hole), and around the back. Tie the ends of each string where they meet at the top of the neckpiece. Or you can attach them with little nails or tacks. Hammer in one set of the nails or tacks at the end of the neckpiece and another at the end of the balalaika body. Tie the ends of each string to its corresponding nail heads. Then hammer in the heads completely.

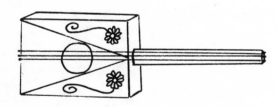

When you play the balalaika, follow the sticks' part. Hold it as you would a guitar—one hand at the neck and the other ready to play. Slap the body of the instrument as you strum the strings. The slap should fit the strong beat of each measure, so that it sounds like this:

SLAP strum strum
SLAP strum strum

The Jewish alphabet is not the same as ours, so the words are written out here exactly the way they sound.

CHORUS

Tum ba-la, tum ba-la, tum ba-la lie-ka (2x)
Tum ba-la lie-ka, shpeel ba-la lie-ka
Tum ba-la lie-ka, shpeel meer a leed.

which means:

Tum bala, tum bala, tum balalaika (2x)
Tum balalaika, play balalaika
Tum balalaika, play me a song.

VERSE 2

May'del, may'del *ikh* veel deekh fraygen
Vos ken vox'in, vox'in oon ray'gen
Vos ken bren'nen oon nit oif heh'ren?
Vos ken vay'nen, vay'nen oon tray'nen?

which you can sing as:

Maiden, maiden, will you explain
What can grow, grow without rain?
What can burn for years and years?
What can cry, cry without tears?

TUM BALALAIKA (Continued)

CHORUS

VERSE 3

Nah'reh-sheh boo-kheh, vos darft dee fray'gen?
Ah shtayn ken vox'in, vox'in oon ray'gen?
Ah lee'beh ken breh'nen oon nit oif heh'ren
Ah hartz ken vay'nen, vay'nen oon tray nen.

which you can sing as:

Foolish boy, should I explain
Stones can grow, grow without rain.
Love can burn for years and years,
A heart can cry, cry without tears.

CHORUS

Note: The combination *kh* is the closest we can come in English to the actual sound needed here. You make it in the back of your throat.

The word "tum" has no actual meaning. It is meant to imitate the strum of the balalaika.

"Stones can grow": The riddle of the stone is the one most people have to think about. If you realize how wind and rain can wash away dirt and grass from around a stone so that it *seems* to get bigger, you'll see what a clever answer this is.

DOWN IN THE VALLEY

The music of the people who live in the Appalachian Mountain country of America has a sweet, plaintive sound that has remained unchanged over the years. Traditionally, it is accompanied by string instruments like the *zither* or *dulcimer*. These old instruments are still popular as background for mountain music.

Making String Instruments

You can make string instruments of your own by following some basic rules of the science of sound:

Sound is caused by vibration, so you need to use strings that vibrate easily (like wire or elastic bands or elastic cord).

The thickness of the vibrating "strings" determines their sound, so you need strings of various thicknesses. Thicker bands produce lower sounds. Thinner bands produce higher sounds.

You need to attach the bands to some kind of base. You can use an empty wax carton (from milk or juice) or an empty wooden cigar box. If you use a carton, cut a center hole about 2–3 inches (5–7 cm) around to improve the quality of the sound.

*waxed carton
with hole
cut out*

If you use an empty cigar box without the lid, there will be more than enough of an opening.

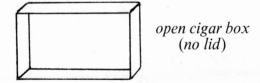

*open cigar box
(no lid)*

Gary is conducting **Tum Balalaika** *with a very attentive group. He's getting them beat-perfect so that when the balalaika player joins them as soloist (following the slap-strum suggestions on page 43), they'll all fit together in rhythm. They've learned the Jewish words, too, so that they'll be able to answer the riddles bi-lingually.*

DOWN IN THE VALLEY

American folksong

Down in the val - ley, val-ley so low. _____ Hang your head o -
Ro - ses love sun - shine, vi'-lets love dew. _____ An - gels in heav -

ver, Hear the wind blow. _____ Hear the wind blow, love, Hear the wind
en Know I love you. _____ Know I love you, dear, Know I love

blow, _____ Hang your head o - ver, Hear the wind blow. _____
you, _____ An - gels in heav - en, Know I love you. _____

Stretch the bands (or elastic cord) around the base and across the opening on the top. If you are using

wire strands, wrap them around. A twist of the ends will close them securely.

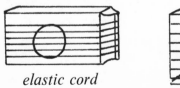

elastic cord

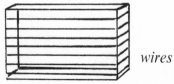

wires

You can attach the wires to a wooden box in another way. Hammer in pairs of tacks or small nails (with heads) along the sides of the box directly across from each other. The number of nails you use will depend

46

DOWN IN THE VALLEY

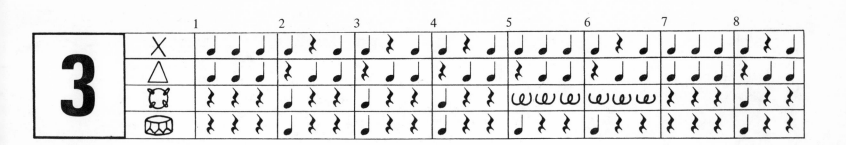

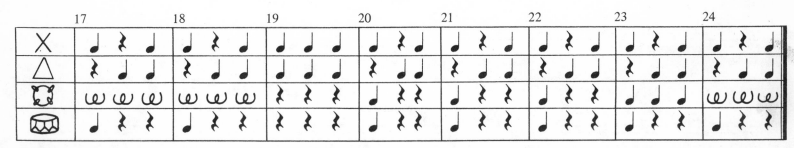

on how many strings you plan to use. To attach the wires, just wrap each end securely around a nail head.

If you are using elastic bands or elastic cord, tie each end in a double knot around the nail or tack heads.

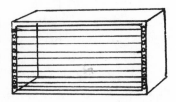

Once you string the instrument, you are ready to play. You can get a good resonating, vibrating sound by plucking and pulling on each string with your fingers. Or you can run your fingers back and forth across the strings in rhythm. You won't get true musical tone from this primitive instrument (you won't be able to play the melody part), but the plucking and strumming will provide a steady, soothing background sound.

47

DEL, DEL SAY-O

African chant from Angola

Look at the drum pattern of this song and the way it repeats. You will often hear this type of sound in music from West Africa. As you can see, the rhythm band score even suggests two kinds of drum rhythms to make the music more exciting.

Songs like this one are sung at gatherings as a kind of sing-along. The whole group, or large parts of it (all the boys, all the girls), sings a very simple set of words like these. Then individuals take turns singing new verses with melodies they compose as they go along. Then the entire group, again, sings the chant as a chorus. They repeat the pattern until there are no new verses to be sung.

The words of this song are a combination of African

DEL, DEL SAY-O

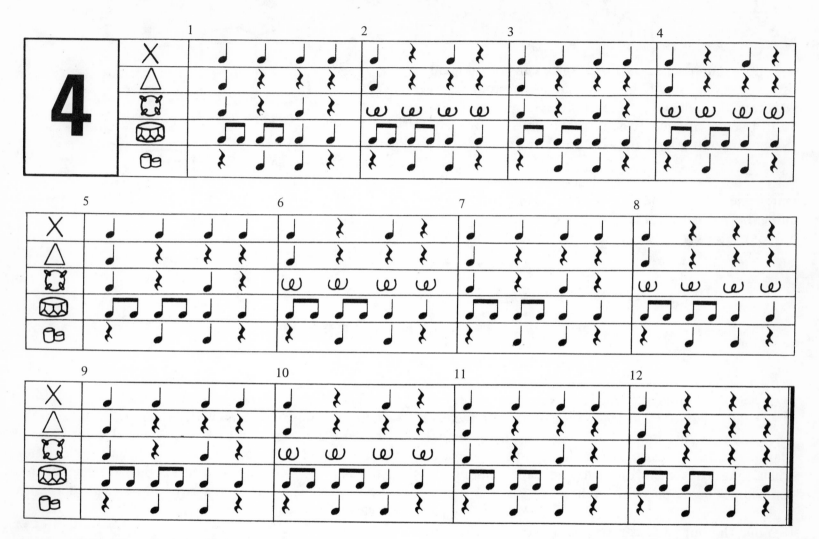

chant and Portuguese, since both are spoken in Angola. The African "Del, del say-o" has no special meaning. It just sets the rhythm pattern. *Menina* means *little girl* and *rapaz* means *little boy* in Portuguese. In this song they chant to each other until their final "farewell"—*adeus* (pronounced ah-day-oosh).

You can add even more flavor by using drums of different sizes and shapes, so you get not only different rhythms, but also different qualities of sound.

If you can't find ready-made drums of different sizes—with different materials covering the heads of the drums—you can make some of your own.

DEL, DEL SAY-O (Continued)

Making Drums

Collect round cereal cartons, coffee cans of different sizes or even small plastic margarine containers. Decorate the outside of the containers any way you want. Use the plastic or cardboard covers as drumheads to beat on with your hands in true African style.

If you wish, you can staple or stitch together the margarine tubs or cereal cartons in sets of two. Many authentic African drums, which are meant to be held on your lap as you beat them, are made that way.

connect here

Two containers of different sizes create another combination of sounds.

connect here

DANSE MACABRE

Camille Saint-Saens, the French composer, wrote this *tone poem*. He used the music to tell an old story of what happened on All Hallows Eve in a cemetery. According to this musical tale, on this night before Halloween, the skeletons dance through the graveyard. Their king leads them on in a wild dance among the tombstones as he plays his violin.

Your rhythm band can turn this marvellous melody —only one part of a much longer composition—into your own Halloween story.

Since the tale begins at midnight—the witching hour —you may want to imitate the sound of a church steeple clock chiming 12 times. The score suggests that you use a triangle to do the job.

Making a Triangle

To make your own triangle, you need a metal coat hanger and something with which to strike it. You can use a spoon or a fork or any metal utensil. Tie an elastic band or a piece of string in a small circle to hold the hanger. You can also use a pipe cleaner, bent to shape, or even one of the covered wires used to close plastic bags.

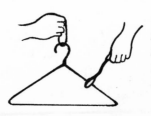

Whatever you use, it should keep your hanger/triangle hanging free to vibrate and produce a tinkling sound.

This group really did start out in the serious mood that befits a spooky song like Danse Macabre. *But their success in scaring some unwary listeners with their final crashing "Boo!" was too much fun to keep them serious for long!*

DANSE MACABRE

From the tone poem by Camille Saint-Saens

Once your triangle sounds 12 times, your band accompanies the "dance of the skeletons," while the sticks imitate the sound of the rattling bones. If you have to use home-made sticks, you can strike together any pair of wooden pencils or mixing spoons.

Keep in mind that you're telling a spooky story with your music. Create the mood by starting out very slowly and getting faster and faster and louder and louder. In Saint-Saens' story, the first glow of the sunrise warns the skeletons to return to their resting places

52

DANSE MACABRE

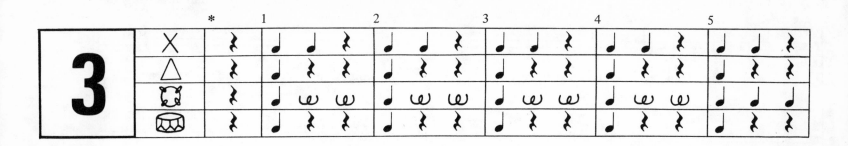

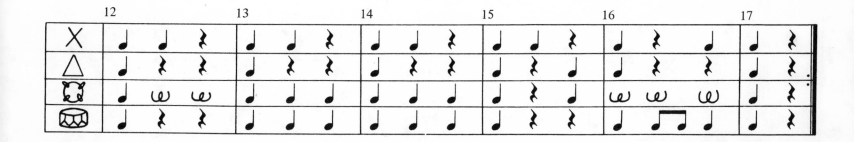

(they are free to dance only during the dark night of All Hallows Eve). You can imitate the rooster calling out the dawn by using a kazoo, if you have one, to make a cock-a-doodle sound. (You'll find directions for making home-made kazoos on page 91 and page 94.)

Then, gradually, slow down and get as quiet as you can, letting the last sound of the sticks be the last clicks of the tombstones as they close on the skeletons who will rest until next year.

THE GALWAY PIPER

Irish folksong

Pip - ing Tom of Gal - way Bay_ will_ get his pipes in tune and play_ and_

folks will come from miles a - way for Pip - ing_ Tom_ of _ Gal - way Bay.

He can_ play both loud and low. He can_ play both fast and slow.

Stamp your_ feet and dance a - way to Pip - ing_ Tom of Gal - way Bay.

THE GALWAY PIPER

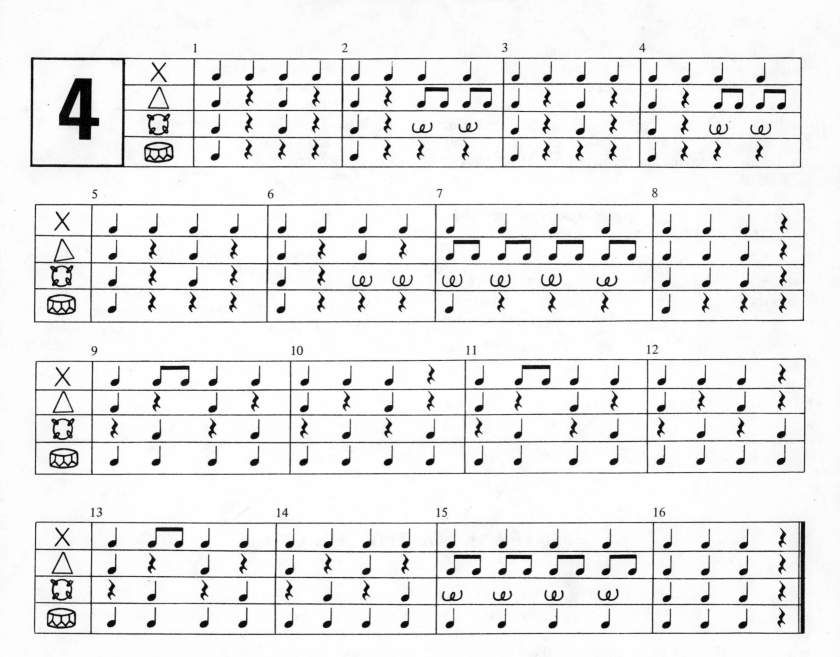

THE GALWAY PIPER

The Galway piper was an important figure at Irish weddings (in the district of Galway, of course). He was the one who "piped the tunes" on his bagpipe for the dances at these country celebrations. He held his old Irish bagpipe (similar to the Highland Bagpipe of Scotland) under his arm as he piped air into it, his fingers moving on and off the many pipes used to play the tunes.

You can dance to the perky sounds of this music with a traditional Irish jig.

Doing an Irish Jig

Two lines of dancers face each other. Each dancer, hands on his or her own waist (thumbs turned towards the back), stands as stiff and straight as possible throughout the dance.

PART I

MEASURES

1   Hopping, in rhythm on your right foot, tap your left heel (toe pointing up) out to the left. Then tap your left toe over your right foot. Do this 4 times, ending with your feet in place.

2   Do the same thing in reverse: hop on your left foot, tap your right heel out to the right. Then cross your right heel over your left foot. Do that 4 times.

3   Repeat 1.

4   Repeat 2.

PART II

5   With hands still on hips and back still straight and stiff, each couple passes on right shoulder side—do-si-do fashion—and moves back to place in rhythm. End (in rhythm) with a left-right-stamp-stamp in place.

6   Do the same thing in reverse: Pass on the left shoulder side and go back to your original position, ending with a left-right-stamp-stamp in place.

7   Repeat 5.

8   Repeat 6.

ENTRANCE OF THE MIKADO

East really met West in Gilbert & Sullivan's famous comic opera, "The Mikado." This British team captured beautifully the flavor of the music of Japan in this selection. It heralds the entrance of the Mikado, the ruler of Japan, with his entire staff behind him. The words were taken from an actual verse which was recited by the Imperial Japanese force when they marched in processions. There had been a visit by this Japanese force to England just before Gilbert and Sullivan wrote this music, and they probably remembered the parades that took place and the gold flags flown during those special events. The words mean: "What is the flag flying before the shrine?"

The rhythm score follows a very strict beat, because the Mikado needs a march tempo to parade in full glory across the stage, impressing everyone.

Make full use of all your instruments for this grand entrance. You'll want to use all the instruments a true Mikado would have had playing in a public procession. Use just one of a pair of cymbals and strike it with a metal spoon or other utensil at the start of every measure. Strike it on the strong first beat, from Measure 1 through Measure 12. Then strike on every beat in Measures 14, 16, 18, and 20. Then contribute one last gong sound to end Measure 25.

Use your finger cymbals, too (see page 35 for instructions on how to make them), for every beat of Measures 1–8. Then let them rest and come back to play every beat in Measures 21 through 25.

You can use the balalaika (see page 42) for this song, too. Japanese music is often accompanied by a 3-string, triangle-shaped instrument called a *samisen*, which is similar to the sounds of the plucking of the strings of a balalaika.

Making a Koto

Another common Japanese instrument is the *koto* and you can make your own. You'll need an empty cardboard or wooden box at least 8 × 11 inches (20 × 28 cm). Arrange 13 strings (or elastic bands or wire) by wrapping them tightly around the box. Then

strum across the strings or pluck individual strings in a rhythm that pleases you.

Strum.

Wrap the strings around.

If you can get silk thread for your koto, use it in place of the strings, as the Japanese do. If you use silk thread (polyester thread works almost as well), try to get a box made of wood and your sound will be more authentic. Hammer two sets of 13 small nails into the short sides of the box. Leave just enough of the heads of the nails exposed so that you can wrap the silk threads around them very tightly.

When all 13 threads are attached and taut, hammer in each nail head all the way, so that the threads stay taut. Then you'll get a springy sound as you strum or pluck the strings.

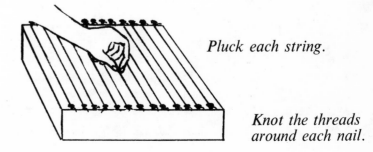

Pluck each string.

Knot the threads around each nail.

ENTRANCE OF THE MIKADO

From "The Mikado" by Gilbert & Sullivan

Mi - ya sa - ma, mi - ya sa - ma   on n'm ma no   ma - ye ni   pi - ra pi - ra

su - ru no - wa   nan - gia   -   na. ____   To - ko   ton - ya - re   ton - ya - re

na!

ENTRANCE OF THE MIKADO

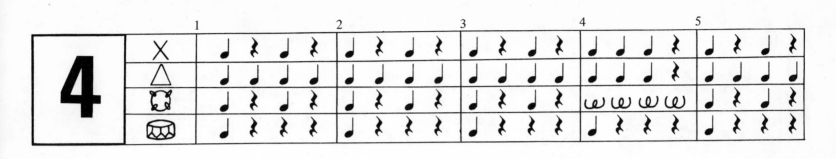

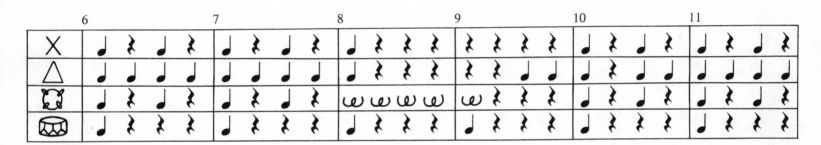

SURPRISE SYMPHONY

from Symphony #94 by Josef Haydn

sf — Sforzando which means "suddenly loud."

SURPRISE SYMPHONY

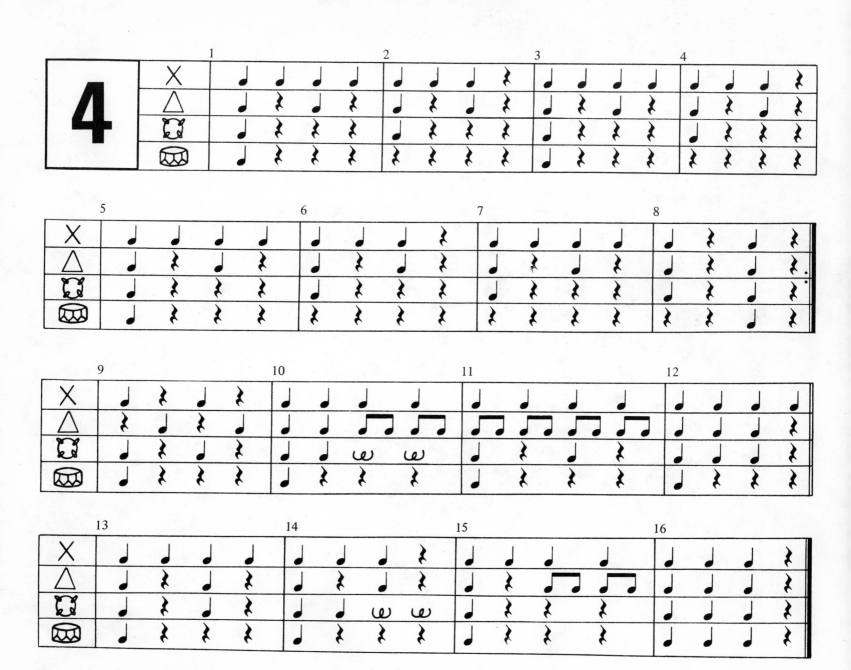

SURPRISE SYMPHONY

The nickname "surprise" was given to this melody because the composer, Josef Haydn, used it to play a trick on his audience. He was convinced that some listeners were falling asleep during his concerts. So during symphony #94, at one spot in the melody, he had the instruments play one chord together—as loudly as they could. This, Haydn was sure, would wake up anyone who had nodded off to sleep. You can have the same fun with your audience.

The score for this music uses cymbals as the "waker-upper," but you can add your own noisemakers. Just follow the pattern for the cymbals. You can use two flat pot lids for cymbals. Hold them by their knobs or handles in pairs and play them as cymbals just as they come from the kitchen.

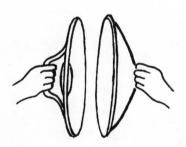

You can get an even louder and more crashing sound by holding 2 frying pans by the handles and striking them as you would cymbals. That sound would wake up any crowd.

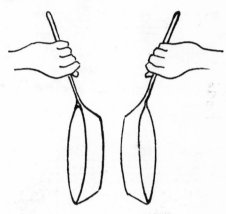

Making Your Own Cymbals

To make your own pair of cymbals, attach empty thread spools as knobs to the undersides of a pair of pie plates (not glass ones!).

Photo on left-hand page: With the author at the piano, the cymbal section is ready to play the "surprise" of this symphony. Larry (in the print shirt) has his cymbals in perfect position to strike. They are close together—one above the other—and will give a good resounding crash as he strikes one off the other and lets them vibrate freely.

You'll get more of the sound you want from a pair of metal plates, but if you hit aluminum plates just right, you can get a good sound from them, too.

POLLY WOLLY DOODLE

American folksong

Oh, I went down south for to see my Sal, Sing-ing Pol-ly wol-ly doo-dle all the day. Oh, my Sal-ly am a___ spun-ky gal, Sing Pol-ly wol-ly doo-dle all the day. Fare thee well, Fare thee well, Fare thee well, my fai-ry fay, For I'm goin'-a Lou'-si-an-na for to see my Su-si-an-na, Sing-ing Pol-ly wol-ly doo-dle all the day.

POLLY WOLLY DOODLE

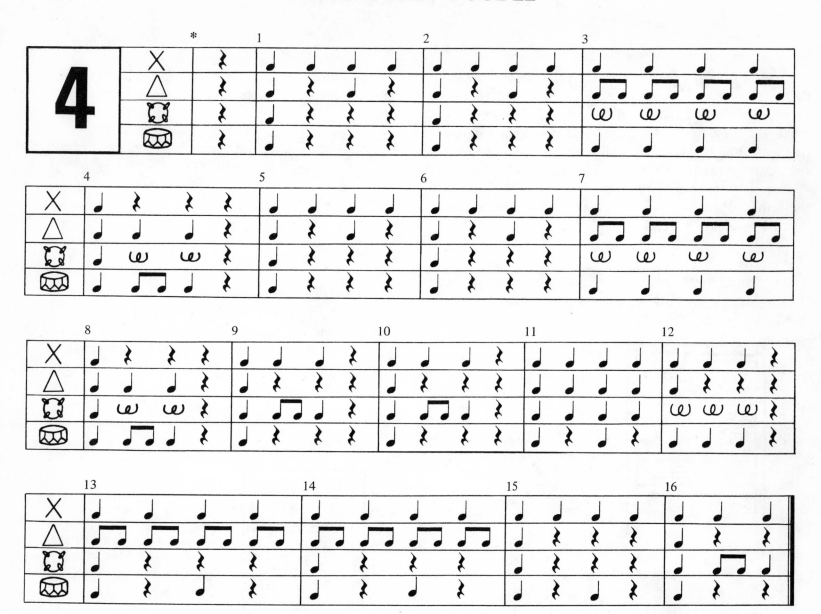

POLLY WOLLY DOODLE

In pioneer days few of the early American settlers had instruments to accompany their singing and dancing at the end of long days of travelling. So they used whatever they had with them. Most pioneer families had a washboard. It was usually made from galvanized tin, corrugated into grooves to get clothes clean. "Musicians" used these washboards, too. They rubbed their fingertips or knuckles along the grooves when they wanted to create a steady beat.

If your family has one of these old washboards somewhere, stored away, you can use it in your band just as they did long ago, thumping out a strong beat for your band.

If you don't have a washboard at home, you may be able to find one in the housewares section of a department store or at a hardware dealer's.

Making a Washboard

If you want to make a "washboard" of your own, you'll need some corrugated paper and some sticks or slats of wood to use as a frame for it. An old picture frame makes an ideal "board" for your corrugated paper. Just attach the corrugated paper to it. Depending on the kind of frame it is, you can tack, staple, nail or glue the paper to the back of the frame.

Attach the corrugated paper to the back-of-frame depression.

If you need to make a frame, cut the sticks to form a frame about 8 × 11 inches (20 × 27.5 cm) and nail or glue the corners together. Cut the corrugated paper about an inch larger on all sides than the frame so that you can attach the paper to the back of the frame.

Nail the border of the corrugated paper to the back of the home-made frame.

HAPPY THUMPING!

SHEEP-SHEARING TIME

It is the sheep shearers' job to cut the wool from the sheep each season. It's very hard work since there are thousands of sheep and each one must be sheared by hand to get as much wool as possible and in as perfect a piece as possible without hurting the sheep. Most sheep stations do not have their own shearers since the work is seasonal. The very skilled shearers travel from ranch to ranch at sheep-shearing time. A good shearer seizes the sheep rapidly, holds it still and works so swiftly that his fingers seem to fly across the sheep's body. They keep to a regular rhythm that helps them cut the fleece that will be turned into beautiful wool products.

Today the cutting has been mechanized somewhat and the "sheep shears" are electrified and cut with a humming sound. But this folksong tells of the old days of sheep-shearing. The rhythm in the chorus is like the clicking sound of the old-time shears. You can use the sticks for this section.

As you repeat the chorus another time, you may want to create the sound of the bells that often hung around the necks of those sheep *not* being sheared. You might sing "Clang, go the bells, boys," in place of the words about the clicking shears. If you have a real cowbell, it will make a flat-toned clanging sound as you sing.

Otherwise, you can use a triangle to get a bell-like sound. A spoon or other kitchen tools will work, too. Use them to strike a pot lid or the cover of a metal candy or cookie container—or the container itself.

Try to find instruments to produce other sounds you might hear:

—Pots and pans from the kitchen or chuck wagon (the shearers must take time to eat)

—Shuffling feet (sand blocks would be good for this)

—A sweeping broom (or even a vacuum or suction broom for getting up small pieces of fleece)

—The sheep-pen gates.

When you've run out of ideas for sound effects, you can change the chorus idea around by singing about the sounds:

—"Baa," go the sheep, boys, "Baa, baa, baa."
—"Move," say the men, boys, "Move, move, move."

and so on, wherever your ideas take you.

SHEEP-SHEARING TIME

Australian folksong

SHEEP-SHEARING TIME

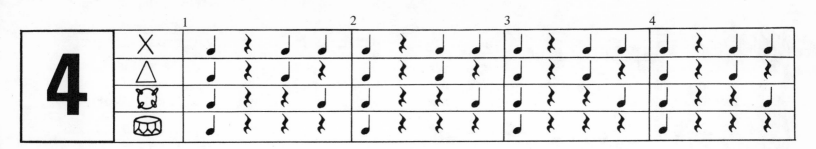

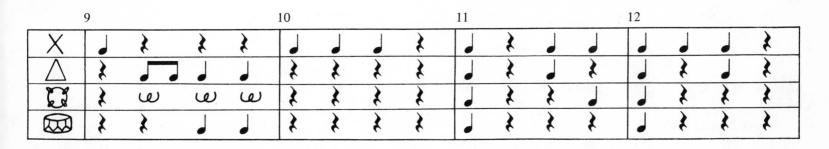

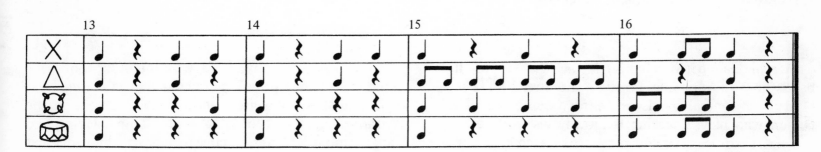

MEECHIE BANJO

Creole song

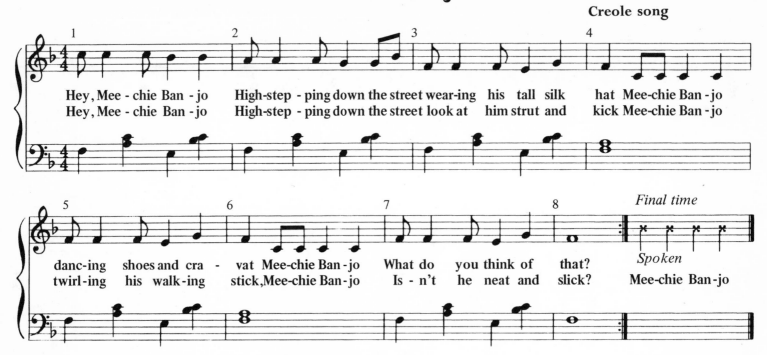

1 Hey, Mee - chie Ban - jo | 2 High-step - ping down the street wear-ing his tall silk | 3 hat Mee-chie Ban - jo
Hey, Mee - chie Ban - jo | High-step - ping down the street look at him strut and | kick Mee-chie Ban - jo

5 danc-ing shoes and cra - vat Mee-chie Ban-jo | 6 What do you think of that? | *Spoken*
twirl-ing his walk-ing stick, Mee-chie Ban-jo | Is - n't he neat and slick? | Mee-chie Ban-jo

Final time

This tune is from the folk music of the Creoles, descendants of the French and American blacks and whites who played such an important role in the early settling of the southern United States. Its syncopation is typical of the jazz music that came out of New Orleans.

Meechie Banjo (Mr. Banjo) is the "leader" of the bands that still parade through the streets of New Orleans as funeral bands or Mardi Gras bands. The person who plays Meechie Banjo always wears a tall silk hat, carries a cane and moves, high-stepping down the street, at the head of the band.

The High Step

1—right knee up

2—right leg extended straight out

3—right foot down.

Repeat these stiff movements with the other foot. This kind of straight-leg walk is very much like the *cakewalk*, and it makes for a great show when everyone in the parade high-steps behind Meechie Banjo, playing and singing along. It takes practice to get everything together in rhythm, but it's worth the effort.

MEECHIE BANJO

Making a Banjo

You can make an unusual banjo for your band with the plastic lid from a 2-pound coffee can or an aluminum pie tin of any size. You'll also need some string or wire and some bells. You can get perfect little bells in a pet shop, the kind they use for hanging in bird-cages. For the neck of your banjo, you'll need a 12-inch (30 cm) ruler or a slat of wood about 12 × 2 inches (30 × 5 cm).

Thread a piece of string or wire through each bell and then through the outer edge of the lid or plate. Space the bells evenly. Then staple or glue the underside of the plate (either side of the lid) to the wooden slat and attach 6 "strings." Wrap a length of the string, elastic cord, or wire from one end of the slat, across the top of the plate/body, around the back of the body, and tie the ends securely. If you're using wire, just twist the ends together to tie off each "string."

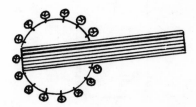

To play your banjo, hold it like a guitar, pluck each string, and plink out your rhythm.

Making a Tall Silk Hat

You can also make a hat for Meechie Banjo. You'll need stiff paper or cardboard and some staples and tape to put it all together. For the top hat part, cut a rectangle about 12 × 20 inches (30 × 50 cm) from the cardboard.

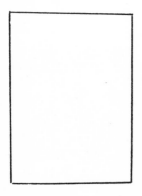

Roll it into a cylinder and staple or tape the seam.

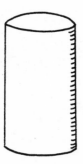

For the brim, cut a circle, about 12 inches (30 cm) in diameter, from another piece of cardboard. Take the cylinder you just made and center it on the circle. Cut a circle from the cardboard the size of the cylinder.

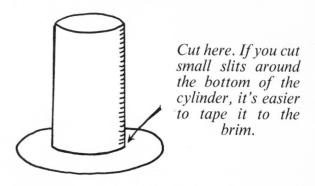

Cut here. If you cut small slits around the bottom of the cylinder, it's easier to tape it to the brim.

Fit the cylinder into the brim and tape the bottom inch (2 cm) or so of the top hat to the brim, on the inside so it won't be seen.

To make the hat more real-looking, you can cover it with black construction paper or crepe paper. If you want to close the top of the hat, just cut a circle of black paper a little larger than the opening of the cylinder. Tape it over the opening and start high-stepping with the band!

Tape the circle over the top of the cylinder. Cut slits in it and you'll be able to tape it flat without its wrinkling.

The song is Ahrirang (*page 74*) *and the band is ready to produce all kinds of clanging, tinkling sounds. Timmy (jingle rattle) and Hae Ryan and Erika (triangles) will play its delicate tones easily. But Stephanie (frying pan) and Hong ("Chinese gong") need to use a light hand as they strike their instruments to avoid too loud a sound. Audra, the conductor, has just suggested that each instrument play 3 beats, in turn, as an introduction, before the entire band plays this gentle song together.*

AHRIRANG

Korean folksong

Far Eastern music uses a combination of tones that is different from the music of the western world. It skips some of the steps of the western scales and creates a haunting, sad kind of sound.

Play this song slowly and with feeling. The singer is desperately lonely for his native land. When he returns to Ahrirang, the mythical mountain, his loneliness will be over.

The Korean words actually tell a slightly different story, of one who has been left by his love. She has gone over the mountain. He would follow if he could, but he has tired feet!

AHRIRANG

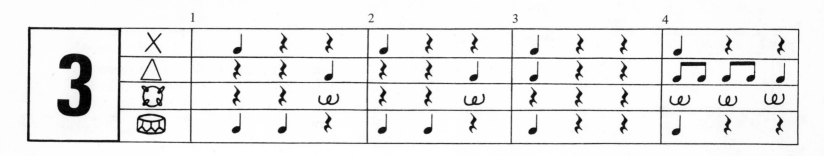

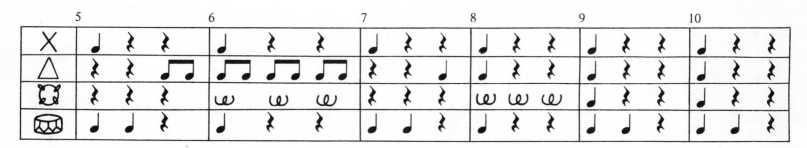

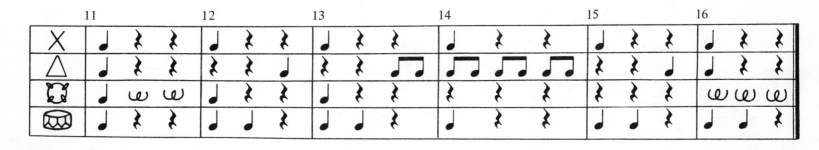

Bells of all sizes—gongs, too—are often used in Oriental music, and you can add an authentic touch by using finger cymbals, too (see page 35).

Making a Chinese Gong

You can use cymbals to create the sound of a Chinese Gong. Combine one cymbal with a drumstick—or some other striking tool—and at appropriate places in the song, gently strike the cymbal with the stick.

If you don't have any cymbals, you can use a frying pan or a skillet for a similar effect.

Some good places for these gong sounds might be between Measures 1 and 2, between 2 and 3, between 4 and 5, between 14 and 15, and between 15 and 16.

SLEIGH RIDE

Russian folktune

Gal - lop - ping a - cross the plains, Rac - ing in the moon - light,

Hoof - beats sound - ing o'er the snow and all the sleigh bells ring - ing.

Hoof - beats pound - ing o'er the snow, oh, lis - ten to the bells — Hey!

Imagine a sleigh ride across frozen plains. The horses pulling the sleigh across the hard-packed snow would probably start off slowly. They would build momentum little by little until they were racing along at top speed.

You can play a similar pattern with your band, starting slowly, building up speed little by little, until you are speeding along fast and end with a final "Hey!" in true Russian style. If you have a conductor to lead this number, it will be easier for the band to stay together, but if you plan carefully beforehand, you'll be able to manage on your own.

You can create the sound of the hoof beats over snow the way radio "sound effects" people do it. For a hollow sound, beating in rhythm, cut coconut shells or rubber balls in half. Take each cut half and hold it in one of your palms, open side down. Then clap the halves onto a table top, the floor, or even your thighs, alternately, each half in turn, to the rhythm of the band.

SLEIGH RIDE

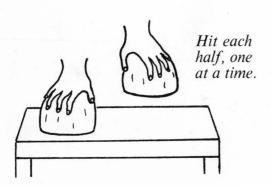

Hit each half, one at a time.

You'll be amazed at how real the sound is. A not-too-bad substitute, if you can't get coconut shells or rubber balls, is simply to slap each thigh in turn.

Play a measure or two of hoof beats as an introduction, before the whole band begins to play. The rhythm band score includes bells (sleigh bells which are tinkling), and you might want to include some of these jingling bells in the introduction. It will add a pretty and true-to-life touch.

LITTLE BROWN JUG

American folksong

LITTLE BROWN JUG

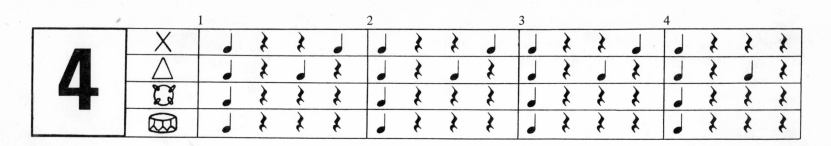

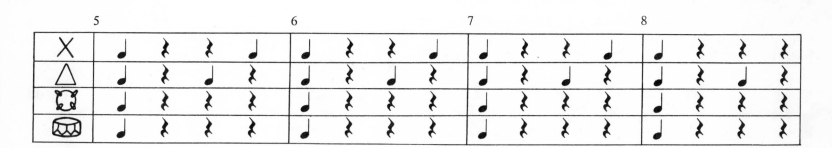

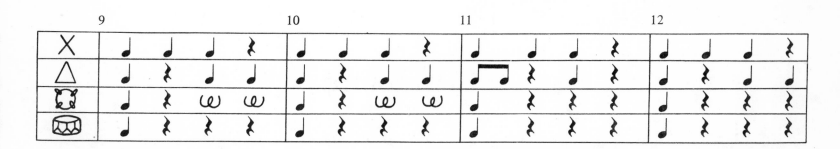

LITTLE BROWN JUG

You play this mountain music from the hill country of Kentucky, Tennessee and Arkansas with jugs and old washboards. Some mountain bands even use washtubs, kitchen spoons and other utensils and cooking equipment.

You can use any large glass or plastic jug, the kind you get when you buy vegetable oil, liquid detergent or cider. If you hold the jug near your mouth and blow across the open top, you'll get a wonderful echoing kind of sound. A glass jug has a more resonant quality, but a plastic jug produces a good sound, too. Adjust the amount of air you blow—and the force with which you blow across the top of the jug—until you get the hollow sound you're trying for. Once you get it, keep blowing air in a good steady breathing pattern to the beat of the band.

If you add a washboard (see page 66), a guitar (add a "neck" to the dulcimer on page 44), or a balalaika (page 42), you'll be able to do it up just right. Slap your knee, give out a loud "hee-haw" and let 'er rip!

MAMA PAQUITO

Carnival time is a time of dancing and singing in most of South America. This song comes from Portuguese-speaking Brazil. You can sing along in Portuguese by following these sounds:

Oh, Mama Pah-kee-toe, Mama Pah-kee-toe,
Dee-ah ah-kah-boo ay ah bahnd kohm-ay-sah
Hay! Hay! Mah-rah-kahs!
Hay! Ray-koh! Ray-koh!
Tem-poh day Kahr-nee-vahl,
Ma, ma, ma Pah-kee-toe.

That means:

Oh, Mama Paquito, Mama Paquito,
Day is done and the band is beginning
Hey! Hey! Maracas!
Hey! Guiro! Guiro!
It's Carnival time,
Mama Paquito.

You'll want to add maracas to this carnival song and you'll find directions for making them on page 8.

MAMA PAQUITO (Continued)

You'll also want a guiro that you can scrape along with the beat.

A guiro is made of wood with rows and rows of notches cut or carved around its center part. Usually 2 or 3 holes are cut into the wood to let sound come out easily from the center of the instrument. A small scraping stick rubbed along the ridges produces a rough-edged sound that fits beautifully into Latin rhythms.

Making a Guiro

You can make a guiro of your own with corrugated paper, the cardboard that is used in packages to protect what is being packed.

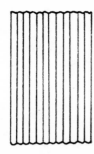

Since the corrugated paper is all ridges on at least one side, you have a ready-made guiro, just waiting to be put together.

Take a piece of corrugated paper about 6 × 12 inches (15 × 30 cm). Roll it into a cylinder and connect the seam with tape or staples. You can also sew a straight seam up the side, if you wish. Make sure the ridges of the paper go in the direction shown here:

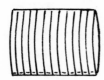

You don't have to cut any holes in your guiro because the natural openings at the top and bottom will allow your scraping sound to come out.

To play the guiro, slip your hand into the corrugated "sleeve" you've just put together. Then use a small stick, a toothpick, or even a pencil (an unsharpened one will keep your instrument much neater than a sharpened one) to scrape against the ridges of the corrugated paper.

one hand inside—one hand for scraping

Making Castanets

To make a pair of homemade castanets, you need both halves of an opened walnut (you can eat the nutmeats inside). Tape the halves together on the top, both inside and outside. Tie a piece of yarn or ribbon, or loop an elastic band around the tape. Then loop this tie around your middle finger. Hold the walnut halves comfortably with your fingers, and clap the shell halves together to make the clicking sound of castanets.

tape *loop*

Place the loop over your middle finger. Use your thumb and finger to click.

MAMA PAQUITO

Carnival song from Brazil

Oh, Ma-ma Pa-qui-to,   Ma-ma Pa-qui-to,   Day is
Portuguese:
O Ma-ma Pa-qui-to,   Ma-ma Pa-qui-to,   di-a

done and now the band be-gins to play.   Shake the ma-ra-cas   and scrape the
a-ca bou, e   a band com-e-ca.   Hey! Hey! ma-ra-cas!   Hey! re-co-

gui-ro.   It's time for Car-ni-val, We'll dance the night a-way.
re-co!   Tem-po de car-ni-val, Ma-ma-ma Pa-qui-to.

You can get the same kind of sound by using empty ring boxes, the kind that open with a hinge. Pull the box open far enough to loosen the hinge. Tape the top and bottom of the box together again; as with the walnut shells, tie a loop around the hinge. Follow the part in the score written especially for the castanets and guiro and click away.

Making a Shaker-Rattle
To make a shaker-rattle, use empty plastic margarine

82

MAMA PAQUITO

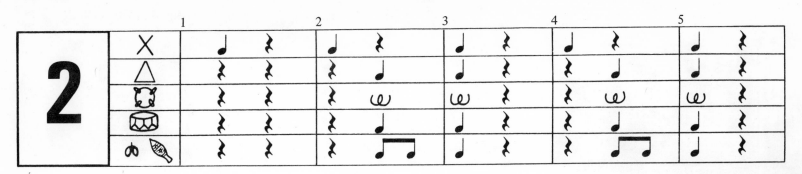

or salad cups, the large size. Cover the writing on the lid with construction paper or paint over it. Then fill the container with half a cup of anything that will rattle—raw rice, macaroni, pebbles, or dry beans. Insert a

pencil or a thin dowel stick into the bottom of the cup and anchor it with tape. Hold the shaker-rattle by the stick and shake it. Follow the part of the tambourines.

Michelle is using a table for support as she scrapes her corrugated paper guiro. If she prefers, she can use the ready-made wooden guiro standing alongside it. Or she can get another kind of scraping sound from the home-made guiro lying on the table top. It's made from a cardboard tray lined with glued-on rows of thick string.

NA'ALEH L'ARTZENU

This folksong was sung by the early pioneers who went to Israel. They sang of their joy in working and settling their land.

One of the more unusual instruments found in Middle Eastern countries like Israel is a very different kind of drum. It is called a *tambour* or *Miriam Drum*. Drums like it were probably played as long ago as Biblical days. In the Bible, Miriam, the sister of Moses, was said to play this kind of drum beautifully, so it was named for her.

What makes the drum different? It is made from clay that is shaped by hand and baked in a kiln or allowed to dry in the desert sun. When the body of the drum is dry, the top is covered with a stretched animal skin, usually goatskin, which is held in place by strong rope or strips of dried animal hide.

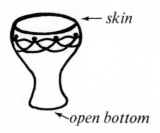

← *skin*

← *open bottom*

Then the drum is tucked under one arm and held in place by an elbow, leaving two hands free to beat it in rhythm.

Making a Tambour

You can make your own Miriam Drum with a clean flower pot made of clay. The hole at the bottom of the pot (meant to allow water to run out) is not as large as the hole in a real Miriam Drum, but it will allow enough sound to be heard when you play it.

To cover the top of the drum, you can use many different materials, from plastic wrap to waxed paper. Hold any one of these papers in place with strong cord or thick elastic bands.

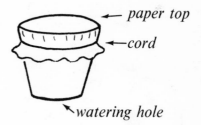

← *paper top*

← *cord*

← *watering hole*

But if you want to make a drum as close to the real thing as possible, take some crepe paper and cut a circle 2 to 3 inches (5–7 cm) larger than the top of the pot.

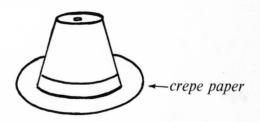

← *crepe paper*

Then stretch out the crepe paper circle as much as you can, being careful not to tear it. Keep the shape as round as you can. Then you attach this "cover" with three or four strong elastic bands to hold it in place very tightly stretched.

NA'ALEH L'ARTZENU

Israeli folksong

You'll be able to carry the tambour with you in the ancient manner if you make a string carrier for it. Take a piece of cord about 1 yard long. Tie a small portion of it around the rim of the tambour. Form a loop with the rest of the cord. Then hang the tambour over your shoulder until you are ready to play it.

To make the drum look more authentic, you may want to attach string or cord in a zigzag pattern along the sides. Thread the cord up through the bottom hole and through the paper at the top, all around the pot.

NA'ALEH L'ARTZENU

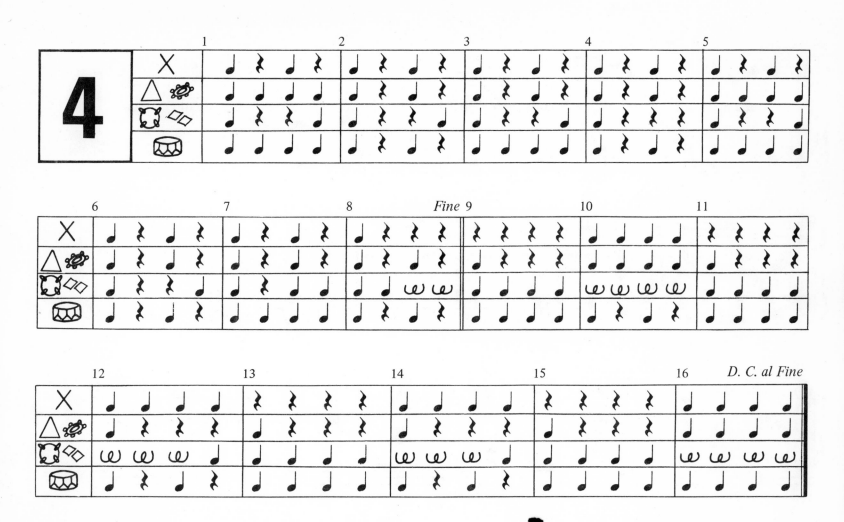

Your tambour will add the hollow drum beat which is native to the Middle East. Play it as you sing the Hebrew words, which appear in the music in transliteration. That means they're written just the way they sound. They mean:

Let us go to our land with joy.
Day of happiness—Day of joy—
Day of holiness—Day of peace.

GET ON BOARD

Afro-American spiritual

turn the page →

GET ON BOARD

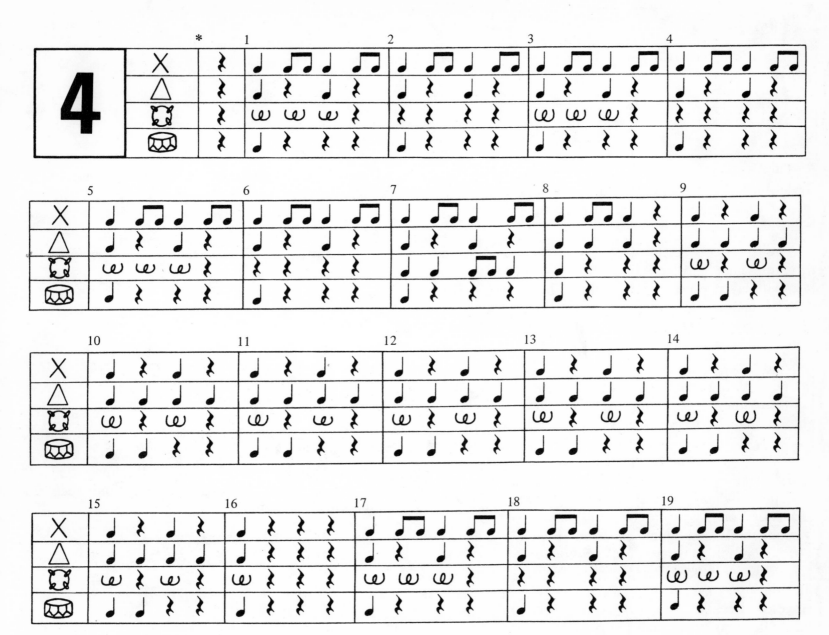

turn the page →

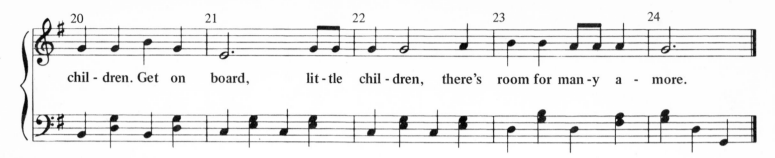

chil - dren. Get on board, lit - tle chil - dren, there's room for man - y a - more.

This well-known spiritual, which grew out of the folk music of black Americans, tells the story of a gospel train bound for heaven. It has room for everyone who wants to "get on board."

You'll see two sections, each with its own distinct rhythm. The first has some very strong beats that cymbal players especially will enjoy. The second, which tells about the train riding around picking up passengers, gives you the chance to make your instruments sound like a train.

Sand blocks play an important part in making these sounds. With a steady rhythm, use them to create the sound of the wheels on the railroad track by rubbing the sandpaper parts back and forth against each other.

Making Sand Blocks

To make your own sand blocks, you'll need coarse sandpaper which you can get from hardware or paint dealers. You'll also need some nails, some empty thread spools, and chunks of wood about 4 × 5 inches (10–13 cm). If you have old chalkboard erasers—the felt kind—they make great bases for the sandpaper. If you use them, you won't even need spools for handles, since the erasers are deep enough to hold easily as you play. Old alphabet blocks also make good sand blocks, though they are a bit small.

Cut the sandpaper to fit the blocks or erasers with enough flap on each end so that the paper will not pull off after you've played them a while. Staple or nail the sandpaper onto the blocks.

wood sand block *board eraser sand block* *alphabet sand block*

These back views show how to fasten sandpaper (shown in black) to the back of the sand block.

Making Rambles

You can add another train-like sound in a very simple way. Just use the plastic fillers that come in candy and cookie boxes. They are the liners that are used to separate the pieces of candy and keep the cookies from breaking.

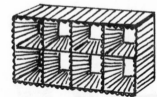

If you twist them in rhythm, you'll get the sound of the train "rolling and rumbling" through the land.

	20	21	22	23	24
X	♩ ♫ ♩ ♫	♩ ♫ ♩ ♫	♩ ♫ ♩ ♫	♩ ♫ ♩ ♫	♩ 𝄾 ♩
△	♩ 𝄾 ♩ 𝄾	♩ 𝄾 ♩ 𝄾	♩ 𝄾 ♩ 𝄾	♩ 𝄾 ♩ 𝄾	♩ 𝄾 ♩
🪇	𝄾 𝄾 𝄾 𝄾	ω ω ω 𝄾	𝄾 𝄾 𝄾 𝄾	♩ 𝄾 ♩ 𝄾	ω ω ♩
🥁	♩ 𝄾 𝄾 𝄾	♩ 𝄾 𝄾 𝄾	♩ 𝄾 𝄾 𝄾	♩ 𝄾 ♩ 𝄾	♩ 𝄾 𝄾

THE CAMPBELLS ARE COMING

The Highland Bagpipe, native to Scotland, is a very difficult instrument to play. You need excellent breath control to inflate the leather bag that holds the air for making sounds. It also requires skillful fingering of the reeded pipes which produce melodic sounds. The "drone" pipes play out a single, accompanying sound. Bagpipers are deservedly proud of their skill and are given places of honor at the head of parades for all occasions, even outside of Scotland.

There are no rhythm instruments with the hollow, droning quality of the bagpipe. The closest you may be able to come to this haunting sound is with a *kazoo*, a plastic mouth instrument into which you hum a tune. The sound comes out vibrating and sounding eerie.

Making a Kazoo

If you want to make an instrument that sounds like a kazoo sounding like a bagpipe (!), you'll need some waxed paper, an elastic band, and the empty cardboard core that you find inside a roll of toilet tissue or paper towelling.

Cut a circle of the waxed paper 2 inches (5 cm) larger than the open end of the cardboard cylinder. Anchor the paper circle in place with the rubber band over one end of the cylinder.

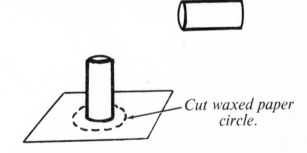

Cut waxed paper circle.

To get the sound you want, touch your lips gently against the waxed paper cover and hum. By experimenting with the force of your humming, you can get a drone-like sound. Use it to play a (short-long)

rhythmic beat at the start of each measure.

THE CAMPBELLS ARE COMING

Scottish folksong

The Camp-bells are com-ing, Hur-rah! Hur-rah! The Camp-bells are com-ing, Hur-rah! Hur-rah! The

Camp-bells are com-ing from yon bon-nie loch,— The Camp-bells are com-ing, Hur - rah! Hur-rah!

The bag-pipes dron-ing a - cross the fen, The drums re-sound-ing be - yond the glen. The

fife and the trum-pet all e-cho a-round us The Camp-bells are com-ing, Hur - rah! Hur-rah!

THE CAMPBELLS ARE COMING

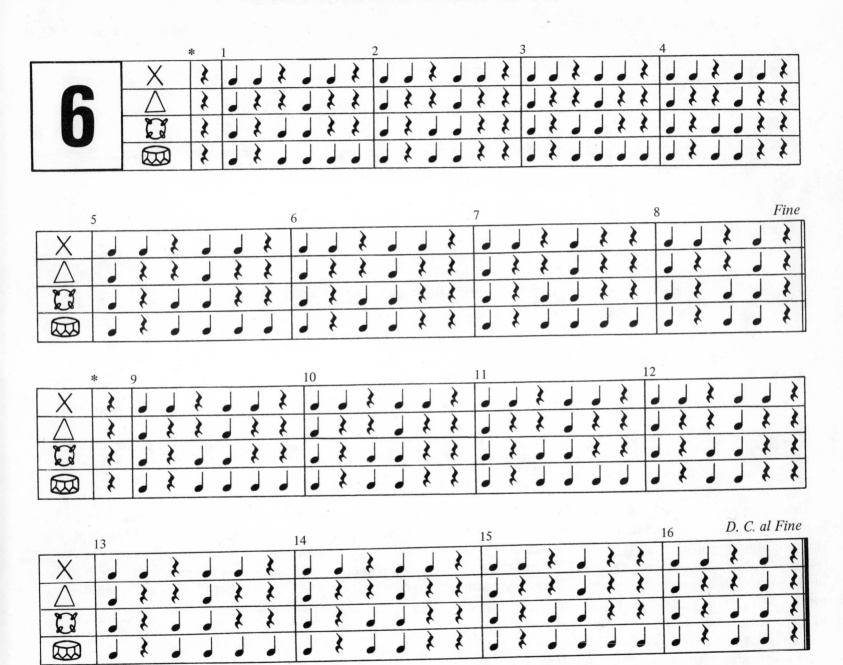

WHEN THE SAINTS GO MARCHING IN

Old gospel hymn

Oh, when the saints _____ go march-ing in, _____ Oh, when the saints go march - ing in, _____ Oh, I want to be in that num - ber _____ When the saints go march - ing in. _____

This song was originally a gospel hymn played by bands returning from funerals in old Louisiana. As the rhythm of jazz music began to develop in this area (especially in the city of New Orleans) around the turn of the century, these bands began to play the old hymn more and more in jazz style. Today Dixieland and all kinds of marching bands play the song as a favorite, and they love to move along to its rhythm.

The melody of the song is usually played by brass instruments, such as trumpets and trombones. There are no rhythm band instruments that sound just like those, because rhythm band instruments cannot play a melody; they can only beat out the rhythm of a song.

But there is a way for you to imitate, a little bit, the sound of a melody instrument to help carry the tune as the rest of the band plays the rhythm.

Making a Comb "Tooter"

Take a comb of any size—a plastic one is as good as a metal one—and wrap some waxed paper around it. Use

WHEN THE SAINTS GO MARCHING IN

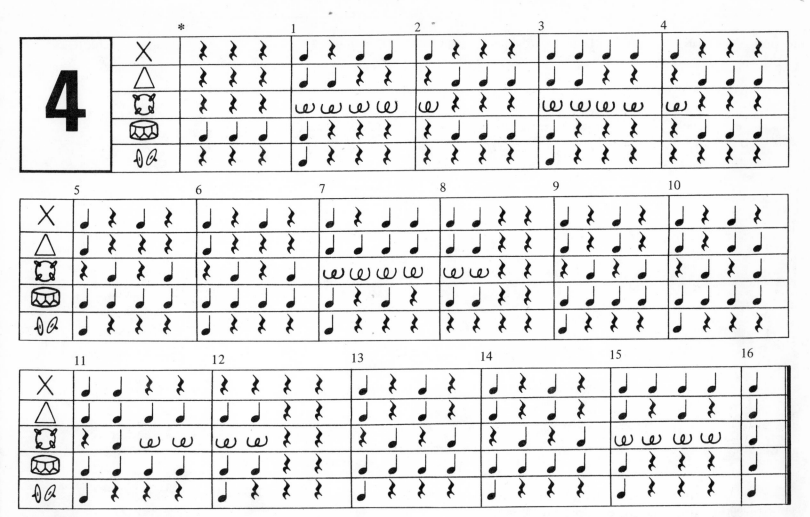

just enough of the paper so that each side of the comb has one layer of paper over it. Hold the ends of the paper with your fingers.

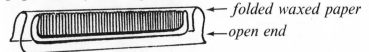

← *folded waxed paper*
← *open end*

Then gently press your lips against one side of the waxed-paper covered comb.

The combination of your voice and the vibration of the waxed paper on the comb, as you gently press and blow on it, produce a "who-who-who-whoooo," which sounds very much like a melody instrument. You'll know you're making the right kind of sound if your lips begin to tickle and tingle as you hum against the paper. That only happens when you're getting the right amount of vibration on the papered comb.

INDEX